MW00723884

Quarterly Essay

1 SLEEPWALK TO WAR
Australia's Unthinking Alliance with America
Hugh White

95 CORRESPONDENCE
Rick Morton, Jennifer Doggett, Russell Marks, Janet McCalman, Nicola Redhouse,
James Dunk, John Kuot, Joo-Inn Chew, Alexandra Goldsworthy, Sebastian Rosenberg,
Sarah Krasnostein

137 Contributors

Quarterly Essay is published four times a year by Black Inc., an imprint of Schwartz Books Pty Ltd. Publisher: Morry Schwartz.

ISBN 9781760643553 ISSN 1444-884x

Subscriptions – 1 year print & digital
(4 issues): $79.95 within Australia incl. GST.
Outside Australia $119.95. 2 years print & digital
(8 issues): $149.95 within Australia incl. GST.
1 year digital only: $49.95.

Payment may be made by Mastercard or Visa, or by cheque made out to Schwartz Books. Payment includes postage and handling.

To subscribe, fill out and post the subscription card or form inside this issue, or subscribe online:

quarterlyessay.com
subscribe@blackincbooks.com
Phone: 61 3 9486 0288

Correspondence should be addressed to:

The Editor, Quarterly Essay
22–24 Northumberland Street
Collingwodd VIC 3066 Australia
Phone: 61 3 9486 0288 / Fax: 61 3 9011 6106
Email: quarterlyessay@blackincbooks.com

Editor: Chris Feik. Management: Elisabeth Young. Publicity: Anna Lensky. Design: Guy Mirabella. Assistant Editor: Kirstie Innes-Will. Production Coordinator: Marilyn de Castro. Typesetting: Tristan Main.

Printed in Australia by McPherson's Printing Group. The paper used to produce this book comes from wood grown in sustainable forests.

SLEEPWALK TO WAR

Australia's Unthinking Alliance with America

Hugh White

The collapse of Australia's relations with China is one of the most extraordinary and consequential events in the history of Australian foreign policy. Just a few years ago, China was hailed as our great friend and the key to our economic future. Now political leaders talk openly of going to war with China – the most powerful country in Asia, our largest trading partner and one of our biggest sources of immigrants, with immense armed forces and nuclear weapons. Not since we faced Imperial Japan in the 1940s have things been so bad between us and a major Asian power. And this is potentially worse, because China today is more formidable and more important to Australia's future than Japan ever was, since it is swiftly becoming the richest and most powerful country on earth. This is the simple fact we must learn to live with. Recent figures from the Treasury in Canberra spell it out starkly. Today China's economy is 19 per cent of global GDP and America's is 16 per cent. By 2035, China will be at 24 per cent and America just 14 per cent.

So what should we do about it? This is one of the most important questions we face as a nation today, and perhaps one of the most important we have ever faced. It is hardly an exaggeration to say that our entire future as a country – our security, our prosperity and, indeed, our identity – depends on how we answer it.

And yet the question is hardly discussed. As relations with China have crashed, leaders and commentators have done little more than declare that we should not give in to China's bullying by complying with its demands. That sounds reassuringly Churchillian, and is plainly sensible as far as it goes. But it doesn't get us very far. It says what we *won't* do but not what we can do, or should do, or will do to manage our relations with China in the years ahead. And that surely is what we need to be talking about, unless we think that we can wait China out. Do we imagine that, if we wait long enough, the Beijing leadership will change their minds and China will go back to being the friendly, undemanding country it used to be and that we want it to be? If so, we are dreaming. That China – if it was ever not just a comforting delusion – is not coming back. This means we have to learn to deal with the assertive, ambitious and, at times, aggressive China of today. So, are we content for things to continue as they are indefinitely, with us quite unable to engage constructively with this extraordinarily powerful and important country? Are we comfortable with the possibility that things will get worse – that we might plunge from open hostility to outright enmity? Do we really believe, as the Morrison government plainly did, that if necessary we should go to war with China to stop it achieving its strategic ambitions? Have we any idea what that would mean or where it would lead? Or do we want things to improve? What could we do, and what price are we prepared to pay, to help that happen? What are workable relations with China worth to us?

These are questions that should have been addressed in the 2022 election. It was, as many people have remarked, something of a khaki election. Not since 1966 have voters heard so much talk about defence and foreign affairs in a campaign. In 1966, it was all about the Vietnam War. This year's election was shadowed by the war in Ukraine and Beijing's moves in Solomon Islands. The Ukraine crisis brought home to us that our problems with China are part of something much bigger – a global crisis of international order – while events in Solomon Islands seemed to bring that crisis close to home. But, tellingly, the underlying questions today are the same as they were in 1966. How to deal with China's ambitions as a major power in Asia? And how far to follow America's lead in doing so?

There is a big difference, however, in how these questions were addressed then and now. In 1966, the major parties offered strikingly different policies. Labor under Calwell and Whitlam wanted to step back from supporting US policy in Asia and look for new ways to engage with China. The Coalition wanted to stick with America in Vietnam and rejected any accommodation with Beijing. Calwell lost the election, but his policies on this were right. In time, both Australia and America abandoned Vietnam and opened to China.

This year there has been no material difference between the two parties' policies on China, and hence no real debate. Instead, there has been a bogus face-off in which both sides used the China issue to score campaign points. The Coalition claimed without any basis that Labor was soft on Beijing, and Labor claimed without any basis that it would handle China better than the Coalition government did. And for all the talk of rising military threats in our neighbourhood, and though the frightful reality of war was hammered home to us every day from Ukraine, neither side took the risks of war in Asia seriously enough to offer ideas about how a war might be avoided, nor about how, if it could not be avoided, a war might be fought and won.

The explanation for this failure is simple. Behind the point-scoring lies a strong bipartisan consensus that the future of our relations with China lies in America's hands, and that we can, and must, rely on America to fix our China problem for us. This consensus has not been reached through careful analysis of the issues and options. It is the product of habit and timidity. Far more than their predecessors in earlier decades, most Australian political leaders, policy-makers and commentators today place immense faith in American power and resolve. They take for granted that America can and will convince or compel Beijing to change its ways so that our relations with China can go back to the way they used to be.

They shy away from the alternative – that America might fail, and that Australia would then have to solve our China problem by ourselves. They are perhaps reluctant to acknowledge the demands that would make of them. That may be understandable, but it is not okay.

Not okay, because we cannot take it for granted that America will solve our China problem for us. On the contrary, as I will argue in this essay, our ally will probably fail us. Americans will find that it will cost them more than it is worth to maintain leadership in Asia against China's formidable challenge. Sooner or later, they will step back from the region and leave us to make our own way with China as best we can. That is not something our leaders can imagine. When Scott Morrison announced the AUKUS arrangement with the United States and the United Kingdom, he memorably and revealingly spoke of our alliances with them as "forever partnerships." But there are no forever partnerships between countries. When the chips are down, allies always do what is in their interests, and that changes with circumstances. When wealth and strength shift from old established powers to new rising ones, declining countries abandon old commitments as costs and risks begin to outweigh benefits. Then their alliances decay. Nothing substantive remains behind the rhetorical facade of alliance back-slapping, such as Canberra's cringe-makingly sentimental and grossly ahistorical talk of our US alliance as "One Hundred Years of Mateship." Then, when a crisis breaks, the facade cracks. That is why alliances so often fail under stress.

Australia is no stranger to alliance failure, as Morrison should have recalled before talking of a "forever partnership" with the United Kingdom. Our first great alliance failed in 1941, at what was, until now, the most perilous moment of our history. In that crisis the UK's strength proved unequal to the demands it faced, and it decided that defending Australia was no longer a priority. Many Australians hold the UK to blame for leaving us to face Japan defenceless. But it was more truly Australia's failure than the United Kingdom's. We failed to see what was glaringly obvious in the years before the crisis broke. The UK was no longer strong enough to protect us from a powerful Asian adversary. It was the British leaders' fault that they kept misleading us, and perhaps themselves, about the new realities of power. But it was our fault that we so eagerly believed that they could and would still defend us, in the face of all the evidence that they could not. And it was our fault that we did not take more responsibility for our own security as a result. If, today, we look for lessons from the 1930s to guide our policy in the dangerous years ahead – as Morrison so often said we should – then this is the one we should attend to most carefully. What we should learn is the need to think a lot more carefully about the problems we face with China, how realistic it is to rely on America to solve them, and what we can do instead.

*

The first step is to understand why things have got so bad. The obvious answer is that China's leaders have trashed the relationship by punishing us for a series of decisions that we have taken which they do not like. They include excluding Huawei from our 5G system and banning Chinese investment in other key infrastructure, calling for an international inquiry into the origins of the COVID-19 pandemic, criticising Beijing's policies in Hong Kong and Xinjiang and many more. But these disagreements are only symptoms of the problem. The cause goes much deeper. It is Australia's decision to overtly, explicitly and energetically oppose China's ambition to push America out of East Asia and take its place as the leading regional power. No issue is more important to Beijing than this. It is one of China's highest and most cherished priorities, central to the restoration of China's power, status and identity as the natural leader of its region, and as dear to China's people as it is to their leaders.

For a long time, Canberra, like Washington, underestimated this ambition, and thus played down the chances of serious strategic rivalry. That allowed them confidently to say that Australia would not have to choose between America and China, so we could continue to rely on China to make us rich and on America to keep us safe. This worked well while it lasted. Canberra quietly assured Washington of Australia's full support if push ever came to shove with China, while our trade and diplomatic relationship with China flourished. The day she was deposed in 2013, Julia Gillard could boast that her government had "strengthened both our alliance with the United States while taking a major stride forward in our relationship with China." It was a fair claim from a leader who had been feted both in Washington and Beijing. She had warmly endorsed Barack Obama's "Pivot to Asia" and welcomed US marines to Darwin. At the same time, she convinced Xi Jinping to describe our relationship with China as a "comprehensive strategic partnership" and to commit to annual meetings of the two countries' most senior leaders.

Tony Abbott followed her example. He was loudly pro-America, but in 2014 he welcomed Xi as an honoured guest to Canberra to address a joint sitting of parliament and finalise the China–Australia Free Trade Agreement. Abbott even praised Xi as a true friend and champion of democracy and made much of the fact that he had visited every state in the Commonwealth, which was taken as showing Xi's special affection for Australia.

It is hard now to say how much this reflected honest delusion on Canberra's part and how much was deliberate duplicity. Our leaders must have known that the foundations of our position were fragile. Those foundations had been laid by John Howard back in 1996, in a conversation with China's then leader, Jiang Zemin. He told Jiang that Australia's alliance with America was sacrosanct, but that nothing Australia did as a US ally would be directed against China. Canberra must have understood that this undertaking would be unsustainable if tensons escalated between Washington and Beijing, because Washington would then expect Australia's full support. Our leaders must have understood that this escalation was bound to happen sooner or later as China kept pushing harder and harder for more regional influence at America's expense. They must have known, too, that the harder China pushed, the more uneasy Australians would feel about living under its shadow.

Did Gillard, Abbott and their advisers see where things were heading and proceed anyway? Did they knowingly mislead both sides, by assuring

Washington that we would support them against China, while assuring Beijing that we wouldn't? Or did Gillard and Abbott really believe that the crunch wouldn't come – that China would keep growing richer and stronger without seriously challenging US leadership in Asia? It was probably a bit of both, as Abbott's famously undiplomatic but beguilingly honest comment to German chancellor Angela Merkel about Australia–China relations suggests. On the eve of Xi's visit to Canberra in 2014, she asked Abbott about the basis of Australia's China policy. "Fear and greed," he shot back with, one imagines, his characteristic edgy grin. That showed, I think, that he knew our policy was built on sand.

It began to collapse in 2017. Three factors contributed to this. The first was change in America. Donald Trump overturned Washington's approach to China. Suddenly everyone agreed that China was a serious strategic rival that must be vigorously opposed and contained, and US allies in Asia were expected to help. Australia was now being told it must choose between America and China. The second factor was change in China. As Xi's grip on power in Beijing tightened and evidence of growing repression in China increased, it became harder to sustain Gillard's and Abbott's benign image of China's leaders. At the same time, China's ambitions became harder to ignore as its diplomacy became more abrasive while its military reach and power grew swiftly.

All this in turn produced a third factor, which was a shift in attitudes in Australia. Malcolm Turnbull had long been more willing than any other senior politician on either side to acknowledge and accept Chinese strategic ambitions, but in 2017 he changed tack and began to focus on China's threats to Australia. In June that year, in a major speech in Singapore, he criticised China's new assertiveness and called out its ambition to take America's place as the dominant regional power. Later in the year, he raised concerns about Chinese interference in Australian domestic politics and rushed new laws through parliament to deal with it. He also highlighted potential strategic risks from Chinese involvement in critical infrastructure. The new tone chimed with the tough-on-China rhetoric of the Trump administration. It was encouraged by some forceful ministerial advisers, public servants and intelligence officials in Canberra. It was highlighted by some eye-catching scandals, such as the Sam Dastyari affair. And it was welcomed by the restive and potentially rebellious right wing of the Liberal Party, which, perhaps following Trump's lead, had begun to swing firmly and noisily against China.

By the end of 2017, Turnbull had repositioned Australia as the most stridently anti-Chinese country in the region, and indeed globally. China hit back by freezing senior-level contacts with Canberra. Turnbull seemed surprised and disconcerted by this entirely predictable response, and in early August 2018 he tried to back-pedal with a major "reset" speech at the University of New South Wales. Two weeks later, he was out and Scott Morrison had his job. At first Morrison took his cue from Turnbull's reset, being careful to soothe Beijing where he could. In November 2018, he pushed back against the Trump administration's hardening line on China, saying that "Australia doesn't have to choose and we won't choose" between America and China.

But his tune changed in early 2020, when, after his disastrous response to the Black Summer bushfires, Morrison and his foreign minister, Marise Payne, stumbled, it seems unintentionally, into a confrontation with Beijing over the conduct of an international enquiry into the origins of the COVID-19 pandemic. Things quickly escalated from there, with each side provoking the other in a classic tit for tat. By the end of the year, China had imposed restrictions on Australian exports worth some $25 billion a year and was criticising Australia for a long list of actions and attitudes it deemed unacceptable. Morrison won applause at home and in Washington for refusing to bow to Beijing's bullying. If China's aim has been to force Australia to change policies on the issues under dispute, then it has plainly failed. If its aim has been to make an example of us, to issue a warning to other countries not to follow our lead, then it has probably succeeded. And, more fundamentally, it has succeeded in goading Australia into an absurd and ultimately unsustainable position. By the end of 2020, bad relations with China seemed to have become an end in itself, almost a policy objective. Provoking China was now seen as proof of diplomatic judgment and strategic resolve, and Morrison repeatedly declared that any attempt to improve relations would be a betrayal of our national interests and an affront to our sovereignty. As if we had no national interest in workable relations with China and our sovereignty precluded compromise on any issue whatsoever. This is the spirit in which he refused even to meet China's newly arrived ambassador in Canberra.

But if 2020 was a bad year in Australia–China relations, 2021 was worse. Already in June 2020, Morrison had launched his government's Defence Strategic Update by saying that Australia's strategic circumstances were more serious than at any time since the late 1930s. He made it quite clear that the primary focus of Australia's defence preparations was the possibility of war with China in defence of US strategic primacy in Asia, and proclaimed a major expansion of capabilities to prepare for that war. This theme was taken up and amplified by Peter Dutton after he became defence minister in March 2021. He spoke often of a real risk of war with China, and said it was "inconceivable" that Australia would not support America in a conflict over Taiwan. Morrison did not go that far, but he conspicuously failed to repudiate Dutton's war talk. Dutton explained his thinking in a remarkable presentation to the National Press Club in November 2021. China's aim, he said, was to subjugate Australia and its region. "They do see us as tributary states," he said. He warned that China aimed to impose its will by the threat or use of force, and that it must be deterred in the same way. Australia's aim, therefore, was to maximise our contribution to the military deterrence of China by building up our capacity to fight in a US-led coalition if and when war came. On Anzac Day 2022, he warned again that Australians must prepare to support America in a war with China.

This provided the setting for the bombshell announcement in September 2021 of the AUKUS deal for America and the United Kingdom to help Australia build nuclear-powered submarines. This was more than a major shift in Australia's defence capability plans. It marked a major shift in our strategic positioning, as Dutton made clear when he said that it was the "most significant step taken by the Australian government in defence policy in our lifetime." Morrison went even further when he said it was Australia's "single greatest initiative" since the ANZUS Treaty. To them, and to the many observers around the world who have hailed it as a historic shift in strategic tectonics, AUKUS marks the point at which Australia's commitment to support America in a war with China moved from the cautiously worded ambiguities of the ANZUS Treaty to something much simpler and plainer and more automatic. Under AUKUS it really did become, in the eyes of the Morrison government, and in Washington, "inconceivable" that Australia would not go to war with China if America does.

AUKUS is thus even more significant than it might seem. Many people assume that we have always been bound to follow whenever America goes to war. But until very recently, Canberra remained determined to preserve a clear sense of Australia's separate interests and approaches in dealing with China. As late as July 2020, Marise Payne went out of her way to emphasise this. Standing next to her US counterpart, Mike Pompeo, she very deliberately distanced herself and Australia from some of his remarks about China. "The secretary's positions are his own," she said. "Australia's position is our own. We make our own decisions, our own judgments in the Australian national interests." Now AUKUS implies a much closer merging – if not a complete identification – of our interests with Washington's in dealing with China. And the big question is whether this will work.

Whether depending on America works for Australia in the decades ahead depends on the choices America makes about its future in Asia. In thinking about this, we should pay attention to a passage written by Walter Lippman. He was one of the people who did most to shape America's thinking about its place in the world in the twentieth century.

> Foreign policy consists in bringing into balance, with a comfortable surplus of power in reserve, the nation's commitments and the nation's power. I mean by a foreign commitment an obligation, outside the continental limits of the United States, which may in the last analysis have to be met by waging war. I mean by power the force which is necessary to prevent such a war or to win it if it cannot be prevented.

This captures an important truth. When we look past the high principles and rolling phrases, we see that any nation's foreign policy is framed in the long run by the calculation of cost and benefit and the balance between commitments and power – and especially the costs and risks of war. No country can or will sustain for long commitments which are beyond its power, or when the costs exceed the benefits. The key question for Australia is how these calculations and balances will turn out for America's commitment to Asia. If they do not turn out right, then that commitment cannot and will not be sustained, and we cannot then rely on America the way we have done for so long. And the closer we look at the contest between America and China, the less likely it appears that they will turn out right.

The strategic contest between America and China is about which of them will be the primary strategic power in East Asia and the Western Pacific in the decades ahead. This is not complicated. America has dominated the region since 1945 and wants to stay on top. China wants to push America out and take its place.

China's motives are simple. It no longer accepts the subordination to American power that it reluctantly acknowledged when Mao met Nixon in 1972. It now sees itself as a great power, and at least the equal of the United States. Like any great power, it wants to exercise a degree of exclusive influence and control over the smaller countries around it, just as America does in the Western Hemisphere – or as Australia, in our small way, aspires to do in the South Pacific. That means making sure other major powers do not compete with it to shape affairs in its sphere of influence. China traditionally claimed and largely exercised this kind of influence over its East Asian neighbours until its position was destroyed by the intrusion of European powers and America in the nineteenth century. It sees the restoration of its status as a great power and its predominant influence in its region as an essential element of its recovery from the humiliations of that era, and what Beijing calls "the rejuvenation of the Chinese people."

China has global ambitions as well. It wants to overturn the post–Cold War unipolar world order in which it is subordinate to the United States. It wants instead to see a multipolar world order in which it exercises at least as much power and influence as America. We in the West may view this prospect with dismay, but in truth it would simply restore the vision of multipolar global order that the United Nations was designed to embody after World War II. That vision faltered when it became clear that there were only two great powers in the post-war world, creating the bipolar order of the Cold War. That order collapsed when the Soviet Union fell, leaving the United States with such a preponderant position that it seemed to become in effect the sole great power in the post–Cold War order. Now that China has risen to equal America in some dimensions of power, and other nations, such as India, are following, the reversion to multipolarity would arguably be both natural and perhaps inevitable.

But it is a big change. The United States has been the dominant power in East Asia and the Western Pacific since 1945, and after 1972 its position in Asia became essentially uncontested. Even so, after the Soviet collapse there were genuine questions about whether this would last. Quite a few

Americans argued that Washington should abandon the global commitments that it had built to contain communism. They thought that with the Soviet threat gone, the United States no longer needed to guarantee the security of Asian allies, such as Japan and South Korea, that were wealthy and strong enough to defend themselves. By the mid-1990s, however, those questions were put aside and a new consensus emerged that America should remain in Asia. That was partly the result of inertia. US policy-makers are creatures of habit, just like their Australian counterparts. More importantly, however, it looked easy and safe. With the Soviet threat gone, US leadership in Asia seemed to face no serious challenge. If true, that meant it could be maintained at far lower cost and with much less danger than during the Cold War. But was it true? Already in the mid-1990s – for example, in Australia's 1994 Defence White Paper – it was argued that China's rise would test that assumption. By 2000, prominent US analysts, including Aaron Friedberg, were warning explicitly of the dangers to come.

But these were outliers. Washington, like Canberra, was slow to acknowledge the scale and seriousness of China's ambitions. Until 2017, the consensus in the US defence and foreign policy establishment was that China had neither the power nor the motive to mount a significant challenge to America in Asia. They assumed that China was too dependent on America economically, too ham-fisted diplomatically and too weak militarily to risk a confrontation with American power, and that it had no compelling reason to want to overturn the regional US-led order which had served China's interests so well for so long. For many years, Beijing encouraged this perception. Its leaders stuck to Deng Xiaoping's famous injunction that China should "bide its time and hide its power" precisely to encourage Washington to underestimate China's capabilities and intentions until it had grown strong enough to make its challenge hard to resist. But even after China dropped this pretence and began to assert its ambitions explicitly, which happened around 2008, it was hard to convince US policy-makers and analysts of what they were up against.

President Obama's "Pivot to Asia," announced in Canberra in 2011, was America's first clear attempt to respond to China's new assertiveness. Obama said then that "all the elements of America's power" would be committed to preserving the US-led order in Asia. But in the years that followed, almost nothing concrete was done. Indeed, the Obama administration was reluctant even to acknowledge that China was trying to expand its influence at America's expense. Obama avoided direct references to China – for example, in his Pivot speech – and his team were careful not to call China a "strategic rival." When they criticised Beijing's more flagrantly provocative conduct – for example, in the South China Sea – it was as a violation of the Law of the Sea, rather than an assault on the regional order and American leadership, which is what it clearly was.

There were several reasons for this curious reticence. US policy-makers understood that relations with China could easily nosedive, and they wanted to prevent that. They put a lot of emphasis on building an elaborate structure of regular high-level bilateral consultations, such as the annual Strategic and Economic Dialogue, to manage things smoothly and avoid crises. They did not want to alarm US friends and allies in Asia, including Australia, by suggesting that they might have to choose between America and China. They didn't want to make hard choices themselves. They wanted to avoid at all costs any disruption to the US economic relationship with China, which, back then, they still saw as enormously beneficial, indeed essential, to America's own prosperity. And they wanted to avoid anything that might disrupt cooperation with Beijing on issues such as climate change and North Korea's nuclear program. Underlying all this was the growing recognition that as China's air and naval capabilities grew, it was becoming more and more important to avoid a confrontation that might lead to a military clash. Washington could no longer afford to assume that Beijing would back off, or that once a conflict had flared it could easily be won. In short, they were not willing to accept the economic, diplomatic and military costs and risks involved in pushing back harder against Chinese assertiveness.

All this should have rung alarm bells in Washington. All these reasons for not confronting China directly – the need to avoid economic, diplomatic or military ruptures with Beijing – were direct evidence of the ways in which China was steadily building up the economic, diplomatic and military heft required to mount a serious challenge to US regional primacy. At the same time, China's willingness to accept diplomatic costs and military risks – for example, in its very provocative island-building in the South China Sea and its confrontations with Japan in the East China Sea over the Senkaku/Diaoyu Islands – showed how determined it was to push the envelope and put pressure on America's East Asian position. So it should have been clear in Washington that things were not as they assumed. Contrary to the prevailing orthodoxy, China did have both the power and the resolve to pursue its ambitions at America's expense. Some key officials from the Obama administration have since tried to explain their failure to take China's challenge more seriously. They say that through the Obama years they still believed that China would change, and its strategic ambitions would fade, as its growing wealth fostered a fundamental shift away from authoritarianism and towards democracy. If so, they were astonishingly naive. In fact, the explanation is much simpler. They were deeply committed to the idea of preserving US primacy in Asia for all the reasons sketched above, but they were reluctant to acknowledge, address and accept the costs and risks of doing so against a rival as formidable as China was turning out to be. They were in denial.

Then Trump was elected, and everything changed. It seems like a simple story: Americans across the political spectrum suddenly woke up to the seriousness of China's challenge and steeled themselves for a "new Cold War" to defend the international system from this formidable adversary. The reality is a bit more complex, because Trump himself was such a complex figure and his administration worked in such odd ways. Trump came to office determined to transform America's relationship with China, but his focus was entirely on the economic links, and specifically on the balance of trade. He wanted America to buy less from China and sell more to it. He was, so far as one can tell, uninterested in China as a strategic rival, for the simple reason that he was not interested in America's strategic role in Asia and globally, and was thus was not worried that China wanted to expand its influence at America's expense. He was happy to abandon America's allies to manage China's rise by themselves. And he certainly did not believe that America should launch an ideological crusade against China's authoritarian political system. On the contrary, he admired Xi Jinping and Vladimir Putin for their strong leadership and flattered himself that he was in their league. He never made a substantial statement attacking China's strategic ambitions or describing it as a strategic rival.

But, unlike Obama, Trump was also unconcerned by the short-term costs of confronting China in a new Cold War. He wasn't worried about disrupting the economic relationship because that was what he wanted to do. He did not want China's diplomatic support on climate change, because he didn't intend to do anything about it. He didn't want its support on North Korea, because he was sure he could fix that on his own, and he lost interest in the whole issue when that failed. He didn't care about putting US allies and friends on the spot by making them choose between America and China, because he didn't value America's alliances and friendships, and he wanted them to make that choice. And he wasn't too worried – at least in theory – about provoking China militarily because he liked the idea of himself as a war leader.

Nor was he much fussed by what his subordinates did or said about China. So it was that Trump's administration developed a policy on China which was quite different from his own. Oddly enough, considering Trump's own antipathy to the US political and policy establishment, his administration team was entirely in unison with that establishment on China. The essentials of US foreign policy have long been deeply bipartisan, and there has always been a lot of consensus among the tight-knit group of people who work on these issues as they move between universities, think-tanks, congressional staff jobs and official positions in Washington. Most Republicans in the club were as appalled by the thought of a Trump presidency as were their Democrat colleagues, and many of the leading figures on the Republican side – the "Never Trumpers" – refused to serve in it. Nonetheless, they responded quickly and unanimously to Trump's iconoclastic trashing of the old guardrails around China policy. The tensions that had built up over the Obama years – tensions between concern about China's challenge and reluctance to confront it – were suddenly resolved, and a new bipartisan consensus swiftly emerged. China was a major strategic rival and needed to be forcibly confronted and rigorously contained.

This new tough line was made official in the Trump administration's National Security Strategy, released at the end of its first year in office, in December 2017. For the first time, China was recognised as a major-power rival. In there, and in the follow-up National Military Strategy early in 2018, countering China's challenge was identified as America's highest strategic and military priority. In the years that followed, Trump's vice president, Mike Pence, his second secretary of state, Mike Pompeo, and his secretary of defence, Jim Mattis, developed and amplified this theme in speeches that painted China as an adversary as serious as the Soviet Union had been. Talk of "a new Cold War" with China no longer seemed a headline-writer's conceit but an accurate description of the new reality. This view swiftly won broad and enthusiastic support across the political spectrum in Congress.

But talk is cheap. By the time the Trump administration left office and the Biden team took over in January 2021, little had been done to show how this new Cold War with China could be fought and won. Just how little was revealed a few days before the Trump team left office, when Trump's National Security Council declassified its secret *Strategic Framework for the Indo-Pacific*. It seems they hoped to show what progress had been made in developing a plan to beat China. In fact, it showed the opposite. It was startlingly feeble. It simply recycled old boilerplate about bolstering alliances, cultivating friendships and strengthening America's military posture in Asia. The implication was that Washington believed that it could defeat China's challenge without doing much more than, or anything different from, what it had been doing for decades. So America under Trump declared China to be its rival in a contest for Asia but did nothing material or practical to win that contest. There was no significant increase in US military capability in the Western Pacific – certainly not enough to offset the swift growth of Chinese forces – and no significant enhancement of America's diplomatic or economic heft in the region. Trump's protection-ism was vividly symbolised by his binning the Trans-Pacific Partnership trade deal that had been promoted by Obama precisely to win back some of the economic influence that had been steadily lost to China over dec-ades. His "America First" rhetoric and the boorish conduct that went with it unsettled allies and alienated friends. His subordinates' scalding anti-China speeches caused even a clingy ally like Australia to step back from Washington's rhetoric. On balance, America's position in Asia vis-a-vis China was weaker when Trump left the Oval Office than it had been when he moved in. So it has been left to Joe Biden to design and execute an effective strategy to defeat China's ambition to dominate our region.

No one would envy Biden his job when he took office in January 2021. At home he was committed to fundamental reforms in education, hous-ing, infrastructure, healthcare and race relations, which together added up to the most ambitious domestic program of any president in decades – all while steering America out of a pandemic. His international tasks were equally daunting. He was committed to confronting and containing the most powerful rival America had faced at least since the Cold War, and perhaps ever. And he had to try to do all this at a time when his legitimacy in office was doubted by a lot of Americans, and the US system of govern-ment faced its worst crisis since ... well, maybe the Civil War?

China did not loom large in the long primary campaign that delivered Biden the Democratic nomination, nor in the presidential campaign in which he defeated Trump. Despite his substantial experience in foreign policy in the Senate, and Trump's notorious incompetence in the field, Biden chose not to talk much about it in his campaign. But as he took office, Biden made it clear that his administration would be as tough on China as his predecessor had been. He spoke of "extreme competition" with Beijing, and told Congress that America was in a contest with China "to win the twenty-first century." His difference with the Trump team, he said, was how he'd do it. Unlike Trump, he'd work with friends and allies. And even more importantly, Biden and his team from the outset placed their domestic policy objectives at the heart of their foreign policy. They argued that the key to winning the contest with China was to rebuild America's society, economy and political system. That would restore America's strength and China's defeat would follow swiftly and easily – and cheaply. All Americans had to do was to make the right choices at home and its challengers abroad would be defeated. It is a view encapsulated years ago by political columnist Charles Krauthammer: "Decline is a choice." But so far Americans have not made the choices required to fix those problems at home, because Biden's ambitious domestic reform agenda is stymied by Republican opposition.

More fundamentally, however, the idea that America need only reform at home to triumph abroad is deeply delusional. It is the delusion of exceptionalism: the idea that America's pre-eminence is founded on something unique and inherent to it, and not on the mundane economic arithmetic of population and productivity which, for over a century, made America by far the richest and strongest country in the world. That arithmetic has been the true foundation of America's ascendancy, globally and in Asia, but it can work for others just as well as it has worked for America, and it is working for China now.

But there is a hard political edge to the delusion of exceptionalism. It holds out the promise that Americans don't have to make any hard choices or sacrifices to defeat China and win the "contest for the twenty-first century." They have been told that they won't have to put up with bad schools, decaying bridges or unaffordable healthcare in order to preserve US leadership abroad. On the contrary, the best way to perpetuate US primacy in East Asia is to fix all the things that are wrong with America itself. In other words, it will cost America nothing to fight and win a new Cold War with China, beyond what it needs to spend to fix its problems at home.

This is an important delusion for the Biden team to foster. They understand very well how fragile the domestic political foundations of US global leadership are. One of the keys to Trump's improbable ascent to power was the disenchantment of the US electorate with America's strategic commitments far from home. Trump wooed voters by gleefully trashing Washington's foreign-policy orthodoxy. He rejected the idea, hitherto held sacrosanct across the political spectrum, that America could not possibly abandon its international leadership role. Anything resembling a return to isolationism had seemed beyond the political pale until Trump's iconoclastic "America First" won a lot of hearts and votes.

And its appeal is not limited to Republicans. In 2020, Biden campaigned on "A foreign policy for the middle class." This slogan reflected, in more moderate but in some ways more graphic terms, the same political imperative as Trump's "America First." It recognises that US voters will reject foreign commitments unless it is clear that they will work to improve the lives of Americans at home. And they distrust the leaders and experts in Washington. They recall all too well the wishful thinking and plain dishonesty of those who argued that invading Iraq and rebuilding Afghanistan were vital to Americans' own security and could be cheaply and easily done. When they understand the far, far higher costs and risks of confronting China in East Asia, they will take a lot of convincing. Secretary of State Anthony Blinken's vague talk of protecting "the rules, values, and relationships that make the world work the way we want it to" will not cut it.

Biden and Trump are not the only politicians to doubt whether these formulas make sense anymore. As long ago as 2009, Obama, speaking of Afghanistan, said:

> As President, I refuse to set goals that go beyond our responsibility, our means, or our interests. And I must weigh all of the challenges that our nation faces. I don't have the luxury of committing to just one. Indeed, I'm mindful of the words of President Eisenhower, who – in discussing our national security – said, "Each proposal

must be weighed in the light of a broader consideration: the need to maintain balance in and among national programs."

Over the past several years, we have lost that balance. We've failed to appreciate the connection between our national security and our economy. In the wake of an economic crisis, too many of our neighbours and friends are out of work and struggle to pay the bills. Too many Americans are worried about the future facing our children. Meanwhile, competition within the global economy has grown more fierce. So we can't simply afford to ignore the price of these wars.

And a little later in the same speech, he said:

That's why our troop commitment in Afghanistan cannot be open-ended – because the nation that I'm most interested in building is our own.

Poignantly, Biden said much the same just last year when he finally admitted failure and brought that sad war to an end.

Obama's scepticism of the Washington orthodoxy grew stronger the longer he served as president. It saw him defy advice by refusing to intervene in Syria after the use there of chemical weapons, and to openly mock the policy professionals in an interview in *The Atlantic*. Many of the same professionals were appalled when Biden withdrew from Afghanistan, though they had failed for over twenty years to define realistic objectives or develop workable strategies there. But now, as America faces its biggest strategic test since the Cold War in Ukraine, even the policy professionals have gone quiet. Not even those who have argued that Ukraine must be offered NATO membership are arguing that America should go to war with Russia to protect it. Few are disagreeing with Biden when he argues that America's response must be carefully tailored to minimise pain to American voters. And that includes most Republicans. Others, led by Trump himself, have even praised Putin's aggression.

Republicans are at one with Democrats in their determination to ensure that America's policies abroad do not cost American voters at home. This is the flipside of the bipartisan support in Washington for a hard line on China which Australia's China hawks find so reassuring. Both sides of the congressional aisle like to talk tough on China, but neither side shows any appetite for the burdens and dangers of actually confronting it. Those who worry that Trump or one of his followers will regain the White House in 2024 miss the point. It doesn't matter who the next president is, or the one after that. No president will be able to compete effectively with China for primacy in East Asia unless it is absolutely clear to the American people that the costs and risks of doing so are truly essential for their security and prosperity. A case must be made for this, and the stakes must be clear. So let's take a moment to clarify the real stakes for America in East Asia.

Why does America need to remain the primary power in East Asia, or prevent China from taking its place? One answer is that losing primacy to China could cost America economically, because Beijing might lock US firms out of the world's fastest-growing region. It is a weak argument to make when Washington is already stepping back from those economic opportunities by decoupling from China. It also overlooks the fact that US economic opportunities are far more likely to be damaged by taking China on as a strategic rival than by stepping back. And even if preserving US primacy did deliver economic opportunities, the question remains what price America is willing to pay, in blood and treasure, to preserve such economic opportunities as might be available. As we will see, those opportunities might come at a cost that far exceeds their potential value.

Another answer given is the need to preserve America's alliances. It is often said – though not by Trump – that these are priceless strategic assets which America must at all costs maintain, and to do that it must remain the region's primary power. That is only half-true. America's regional alliances will quickly dissolve if Washington loses primacy in East Asia. Tokyo's confidence in the US guarantee to defend Japan depends on the clear preponderance of US military power over any credible adversary. That confidence would soon crumble if America loses regional primacy, and so too would the alliance itself. But how much would that matter to America? The consensus in Washington holds that it would be a terrible blow, because they have got so used to thinking of America's alliances as a strategic priority in their own right – as ends in themselves, in other words. That is a mistake – a classic confusion of means with ends. Alliances are never ends in themselves. They are simply tools to achieve policy objectives. America's alliances in Asia have never been anything more than a means to sustain America's strategic position in Asia. If there is no compelling reason to sustain that position, then there is no need to maintain the alliances. It makes no sense to put things the other way round and argue that the position must be sustained to preserve the alliances.

A more coherent reason is that leadership in East Asia is essential to global leadership. Most of Washington remains committed to this post–Cold War vision of a global order founded upon America as the world's leading power. But that vision is not viable, and never was. It is challenged not just in East Asia, but also in the Middle East and Europe. It makes no sense to incur huge costs and risks in East Asia to preserve a global leadership position that cannot be sustained anyway.

That leaves one potentially compelling reason for America to defend its primacy in East Asia. From assuming that China was too weak to bid for primacy in its own backyard, many people have flipped to the other extreme. Now they are convinced that China's global ambitions go further than becoming an equal power in a multipolar global order. They think it wants to rule the world as the leading power. If it succeeds in dominating East Asia, it will be poised to achieve this ambition, supported by other authoritarian states, such as Russia. It could then impose its political values and system globally, including in America, and even threaten America with direct military attack. They therefore believe that China's ambitions in East Asia pose a potential direct threat to America itself. If so, Washington has very compelling reasons to resist.

Are these fears valid? Might China grow so strong that it could attain the kind of global primacy America has failed to achieve? No doubt some people in Beijing, including perhaps some senior leaders, dream such dreams. The question is how likely their dreams are to be realised. Throughout history, the leaders of powerful states have dreamed of "ruling the world." None has ever succeeded. No country or coalition has ever ruled the world, not even the United States at the summit of its power in the 1990s. America's "unipolar moment" was never more than a moment, because it was never strong enough to impose its vision of order on unruly regions and ambitious rivals. That was so even though America at its peak commanded a far greater proportion of global power than China ever will. China has risen faster than any other country, but it has not risen alone. Many other powers are rising too, so that in the decades ahead any country that seeks global hegemony will face a lot of formidable rivals. If China wants to rule the world, it will have to overcome America, India, Europe and Russia. First of all, it would need to dominate Eurasia.

Russia is important here. Much of the alarm about China's global ambitions is fed by fears that Russia and China have formed a deep and enduring alliance to take over the world together. This is a serious misreading both of the global distribution of power and of their current relationship. Even acting in perfect unison, China and Russia together would still not be strong enough to rule the world. In raw economic terms, their combined GDP will remain far below the combined GDPs of India, America and Europe. And there is almost no chance that they will act together. Their strategic goals coincide today because Russia, like China, wants to reassert its traditional status as a great power after a period of weakness and humiliation. Beyond that there is little to draw them together and much to separate them, and the natural rivalry between neighbouring great powers will eventually and increasingly predominate. Russia, as the weaker power, will be intent on not falling under Chinese hegemony, which is no more appealing to Russians than American hegemony. And Russia will remain very formidable, if only because of its nuclear arsenal. India is important too. In the decades ahead, it will have the world's second-largest economy. It will be strong enough to prevent China dominating both the so-called Indo-Pacific region and Eurasia. And then there is Europe, which has great potential strategic power and will be equally determined to prevent China dominating Eurasia.

All this matters because a Eurasian hegemon is America's strategic nightmare, and forestalling that risk has always been the primary reason for America to abandon isolationism and commit itself strategically beyond the Western hemisphere. The United States is inherently a very secure country. It fears no threats from its neighbours in the Americas, and it is protected from more distant powers by its own immense resources, by the two vast oceans which separate its hemisphere from the rest of the world and, since the 1950s, by its formidable nuclear arsenal. It could only ever be threatened directly by an adversary that was so much more powerful than the United States that it could overcome all these, and American strategists have long recognised that this could only be even remotely possible for a power that dominated the whole of Eurasia.

The architect of America's containment strategy at the start of the Cold War, George Kennan, put this succinctly in 1950: "It was essential to us ... that no single continental land power should come to dominate the entire Eurasian land mass." That mattered so much not just because such a power would control far more material strength than America, but because its power would not be balanced and limited by strong rivals closer to its heartland. Without threatening neighbours, it would be able to focus all its power on America – just as America, lacking any neighbouring rivals in the Western hemisphere, has been able to engage itself so fully in more distant commitments in Europe, the Middle East and Asia.

Isolationism made perfect sense for America throughout the nineteenth century because there was no credible chance that a Eurasian hegemon might emerge, thanks to the relatively stable balance among the European great powers. But that changed in the early twentieth century, and by 1917 the collapse of Imperial Russia seemed to offer Germany a chance. If it could defeat France and Britain in the west, as it seemed poised to do, it could turn east again and expand though Russia towards India and the Far East. At that point, America abandoned isolationism to throw its weight against the would-be hegemon. It did the same in late 1941, when Nazi Germany dominated Europe, the Soviet Union seemed about to fall and Britain looked set to follow, while its Axis ally Japan was poised to dominate East Asia and perhaps even India. And the same fear returned in the late 1940s, when the Soviet Union seemed poised to dominate the whole of Eurasia. It already occupied Eastern Europe and threatened a weakened and vulnerable Western Europe. It was pushing southwards into the Middle East. It seemed to dominate the new communist regime in China and was apparently well placed to expand its influence through strong communist movements in newly independent India, decolonising South-East Asia and even Japan. Kennan made clear that this was the threat that America's Cold War containment strategy was designed to counter. America's "entire security as a nation," he wrote, depended on meeting and defeating Moscow's Eurasian ambitions.

None of these three dangerous scenarios materialised, but that does not mean the menace was not real each time. These bids for Eurasian hegemony were only defeated because America intervened to counter them. If China, having dominated East Asia, had a serious chance of going on to dominate Eurasia, then America would have very compelling reasons to block its ambitions in East Asia. There would be a close analogy with America's Cold War policy in Europe: it was determined to stop Moscow dominating Western Europe because that would have led to it dominating Eurasia. But does China have that chance?

Even with an economy and a technology base substantially larger than America's, and even if it can dominate East Asia, China will not have the power to project and sustain across huge distances the massive forces needed to mount any kind of conventional military attack on America. Nor would it ever be able to overmatch and neutralise America's nuclear forces. Whatever happens, America will remain the world's second- or third-largest economy. The strength that provides, combined with its superb natural geographic defences, will keep it safe from China, unless China can dominate Eurasia. Only then would it command a material resource base big enough to overwhelm American conventional defences and – just conceivably – overmatch and neutralise its nuclear forces. And only then would it be free of rivals closer to home, which would allow it to focus its power on America. This means that America only has a truly vital imperative to prevent China coming to dominate East Asia if there is a credible chance that it could go on from there to dominate the whole of Eurasia, as Imperial Germany, Nazi Germany and the Soviet Union all seemed poised to do.

The chances of that seem very low. The big difference between our world and the worlds of 1917, 1941 and 1950 is that, as we have seen, power today is much more evenly distributed around Eurasia than it was in the twentieth century, which makes it even harder to dominate. In 1950, for example, the Soviet Union was by a vast margin the strongest power, and the only nuclear power, in Eurasia. In the decades ahead, China would have to subjugate Russia, India and Europe to dominate Eurasia. All of them would be sure to resist to the utmost of their strength, all of them are nuclear powers – and all of them could call on the support of America if there was a serious danger that China might overpower them. This all makes it very unlikely indeed that Chinese domination of East Asia would lead to Chinese hegemony over Eurasia, which in turn means there is no compelling reason why America must prevent China dominating East Asia to ensure its own security. And as we will see, without that kind of imperative – the kind that drove them in the great strategic contests of the twentieth century – Americans are unlikely to shoulder the costs and risks of containing China's ambitions in East Asia.

Thinking things through

Competing with China for primacy in East Asia is by far the most serious strategic commitment America has undertaken since the Cold War. And yet Washington has launched into it with no clear idea of what would count as winning, how it could be won, how much it will cost and why winning really matters. This would seem almost unbelievably foolish and irresponsible if it did not sound so familiar. This is what happened when Washington launched America into Afghanistan and Iraq in the 2000s, and indeed into Vietnam in the 1960s.

There is a pattern here of US incompetence which we should not overlook. In Canberra, they tend to assume that the American political and policy machine gets things right, and to take what they say at face value. But when the stakes for us are so high – far higher than in those previous debacles – we cannot afford to assume that our allies know what they are doing. We should do our due diligence and decide for ourselves if what Washington is saying or doing really stacks up and makes sense. And the closer we look, the worse things appear.

The problems start with the most fundamental question: what exactly is Washington trying to achieve? Does it aim to preserve the old regional order, with America as the leading power in East Asia, so that things stay essentially as they have been for the past fifty years? Or does it aim lower, seeking instead to retain a major strategic role, but not retaining the primacy that it has enjoyed for so long? Or to put it another way, does it want to remain the dominant power, or does it simply want to stop China becoming the dominant power, by keeping a strong role for itself? Washington has no definite answer to these questions.

Some voices, especially on the Republican side, like to talk of retaining primacy. The Trump administration's classified *US Strategic Framework for the Indo-Pacific*, released just before it left office in January 2021, was quite unambiguous. Its very first words posed the question for US policy as "How to maintain US strategic primacy in the Indo-Pacific region."

The current administration has been less explicit, but the trend of its thinking is becoming clear. Two prominent members of the incoming Biden team wrote – also in January 2021 – that Washington's policy in Asia should "start by moving away from its singular focus on primacy." They argued that America should aim to balance China's power in Asia, and suggested the European strategic order of the nineteenth century as a model for the order that America might seek to foster in Asia. That thinking was reflected in the administration's curiously low-key *Indo-Pacific Strategy*, which was very quietly slipped out in February 2022.

This way of seeing the primary US objective in Asia has support among some Republican thinkers too. Michael Green, in his superb recent history of America's long strategic engagement in Asia, wrote that "the one central theme" has been "that the United States will not tolerate any other power establishing exclusive hegemonic control over Asia or the Pacific." And Elbridge Colby, who has written the most sophisticated contemporary account of US strategy towards China, argues that America's primary objective in Asia should be to prevent Chinese hegemony, not perpetuate America's. That means staying in Asia to balance China, not to dominate it.

Some years ago this made good sense. I argued in my first Quarterly Essay, *Power Shift*, in 2010, and the subsequent book, *The China Choice*, that America should look for a way to share power with China in Asia. But there are two problems with that aim today. The first is in Washington, where there remains a deep instinctive attachment to the idea of American primacy as the only possible basis for US strategy in Asia. The alternative of sharing power in any meaningful way with China in a European-style balance-of-power or concert-of-power system must necessarily mean treating China as an equal. When I suggested that a decade ago, this idea was greeted in Washington with polite bewilderment at best, and often with uncomprehending disbelief. While some serious thinkers such as Green and Colby may now have begun to warm to the idea, there is little sign that Washington as a whole has started to think this way. Nor is there any sign that they have begun to think through what it would look like, how it would work, what it would mean for US allies and how it could be sustained. Those who have argued for this approach – including our own Kevin Rudd – have seriously underestimated the concessions that would have to be made to China to make it work. They expect, for example, that China might agree to ease pressure on Taiwan if America abides more strictly by the One China policy. That might work if China's aim was to preserve the status quo there, but China wants much more than that. It wants Taiwan back, and it will not accept an American strategic presence in Asia if America does not accept that – which no one in Washington is prepared to do, because to do so would be to surrender US primacy. And no one is willing to contemplate that. In short, there is no coherent vision in Washington of any US role in Asia other than primacy.

More broadly, while Rudd's proposals for "managed strategic competition" suggest measures to reduce the risk of conflict over flashpoints such as Taiwan and the South China Sea, they do not address the underlying differences between America and China over strategic leadership in East Asia. They assume that China might accept America's strategic presence in Asia in order to reduce the risk of war. But there is no sign of that. On the contrary, China wants to use the risk of war to force America out of the region – just as America hopes the risk of war will compel China to accept US primacy.

The second problem is in Beijing. America might not know what it wants, but China does. It wants America right out of Asia as a strategic power. A decade ago, when China was weaker and America seemed stronger, Beijing might have been persuaded to compromise and allow America to stay in the region as a balancing rather than dominant power. But today it has a better hand, so it has little reason to compromise now and even less reason to do so in the years to come. It has no interest in a deal, so America will find it as hard to keep a balancing role in Asia as it will to preserve primacy. Washington often forgets that the adversary has a vote.

The reality is that America has no clear and settled objective in its contest with China. Slogans such as "a free and open Indo-Pacific" merely try to mask this critical omission. In truth, however, America aims to retain primacy. There is no model of a new role for America in the new Asia of the twenty-first century, because sharing power in the complex quadrilles of traditional power-political diplomacy is just not what America does. Instead it confronts China in a stark and brutal zero-sum contest for power and influence.

What kind of contest?

In Washington, the contest for Asia is seen as a complex competition with economic, diplomatic, ideological and military dimensions, and there is an aura of confidence that this gives America a lot of opportunities and advantages. This is wrong in two ways. First, because America's position is much weaker across these areas than it appears. And second, because one dimension – the military dimension – counts far more than all the others, and here its position is very weak indeed.

Take the economic question first. Americans often say that this is the primary dimension of the contest with China. Which country will be the chief power in Asia, they suggest, will be decided by which has the strongest economic links with the widest range of East Asian countries. They realise that China's economic weight is a key asset: its leading place in the regional economy bolsters its claim to diplomatic and strategic leadership, while America's declining importance to the region's economy undermines its own claims. They hope that they can reassert strategic leadership by reclaiming economic pre-eminence. But that is not going to happen, because China has already won the contest. Washington and Canberra often suggest that China's growing economic clout flows from the Belt and Road Initiative (BRI), which seems designed by Beijing to build influence by fostering dependency. But the real source of China's regional economic heft is much deeper and broader than the BRI programs. It springs from the very nature of the Chinese economy: its sheer scale and dynamism, its proximity, its openness and the way its structure offers such huge opportunities for trade in both manufactures and raw materials. These have all made it the most important trading partner for every country in Asia, and the best prospect for new opportunities in the future; America cannot match that even if it tries.

And it is not trying. Under Obama, Washington negotiated a regional trade deal – the Trans-Pacific Partnership – that was supposed to help rebuild America's economic place in Asia. It fell victim to America's sharp bipartisan swing to protectionism. Obama never sent it to the Senate for ratification. Hillary Clinton, as the Democratic candidate, vowed to abandon it during the 2016 presidential election campaign, and Trump did so in his first week in office. The Biden administration has no intention of doing any different. It has announced a new Indo-Pacific Economic Framework but has ruled out any opening of US markets. It has talked up plans to counter the BRI by investing in Asian infrastructure, but the numbers are small, and little has happened. Washington will not win the contest for Asia on the economic front.

At first glance, the diplomatic front looks more promising. Washington talks a lot about the Quad – the grouping of India, Japan, Australia and

America – as a highly effective counter to China's bid for regional leadership. It is hard to see why, because the Quad does not actually do anything except meet. Its summits have issued impressive-sounding commitments to cooperation on all kinds of issues – vaccines, climate change, technology, maritime security, cybersecurity, quality infrastructure, supply-chain resilience, counterterrorism, disaster response and countering disinformation – and "working groups" have been announced. But nothing concrete has been delivered. Many of the working groups have not even met. The idea is that the Quad, by offering an example of successful cooperation to tackle regional problems, will highlight the advantages of an open, liberal-democratic, rules-based regional order as an alternative to Chinese hegemony. But it is hard to see how it does that with no real runs on the board. If anything, it sends the opposite signal: that while these four countries meet and talk about a rules-based regional order, China's power and influence just keeps growing. So really it is not clear how the Quad is supposed to help America beat China.

A more charitable view might be that the Quad's unfulfilled action plan is not what really matters. Instead, it is the fact that these four countries' willingness to get together shows that they are united in their determination to resist China's ambitions and prevent it dominating East Asia. But is that so? Certainly all four Quad members are worried about China, but their worries are very different, and so are their ideas of what should be done about it. India, especially, is the odd one out in the Quad, and that matters because India is really what the Quad is about. Japan's and Australia's alliances with America have long bound them to support US strategic primacy in East Asia. The Quad's big idea was to add India's formidable size and weight to their side of the scales to counterbalance China. But is that truly what is happening? That is the assumption embedded in the concept of the "Indo-Pacific region," which both Washington and Canberra have now embraced in place of the old "Asia-Pacific" as their official way of describing the region we live in.

The change is significant. The "Indo-Pacific" lumps East Asia and the Western Pacific together with South Asia and the Indian Ocean in one region, which seems to bring India into the strategic system that China and America are competing over, and suggests that India will help America dominate that region, or stop China dominating it. But changing the way we look at the map does not change realities on the ground. India will always be determined to prevent China dominating South Asia and the Indian Ocean, because India is committed to making that region its own sphere of influence. It has much less interest – in fact, probably no interest at all – in preventing China from dominating its backyard in East Asia and the Western Pacific – as long as China stays out of India's backyard. And that means India's interests and objectives in relation to China are very different from America's. And so too, in different ways, are Japan's. The lack of genuinely convergent approaches to the problem of China is plain in the communiqués that are issued from Quad meetings: China is hardly mentioned, for the simple reason that they cannot agree what to say. And the extent of India's commitment to Washington's vision of a rules-based international order was cruelly exposed by Delhi's refusal to join its Quad partners in condemning Russia's invasion of Ukraine.

So, as a US asset in the diplomatic contest with China, there is a lot less to the Quad than meets the eye. What of Southeast Asia? Washington assumed that as China grew more powerful and threatening, its smaller neighbours would automatically cling more closely to America, and US policy-makers tried to nudge them along by talking up China's bully-ing in the South China Sea. But it hasn't worked. The Southeast Asians are acutely aware of China's ambitions and anxious about falling too far under its shadow. But they have no interest at all in taking America's side against China in a new Cold War. Singapore is America's closest partner in the region, but its prime minister, Lee Hsien Loong, has made this very clear. In 2020, he wrote that China and America "must work out a modus vivendi" in Asia. It does not help that the Biden administration has at times framed the rivalry with China in ideological terms as a stark contest between democracy and authoritarianism. That sells poorly in Southeast Asia, where these questions take on subtle shades of grey. When Biden convened a "Summit for Democracy" in December 2021, many important Southeast Asian countries, including Singapore, were not invited. Whoops.

It seems that the Biden team has now come to understand this. Secretary of State Blinken finally found time to visit Southeast Asia late in 2021. While there, he said that America does not ask Southeast Asian countries to make a choice between America and China – which is absurd, of course, because that is exactly what he wants them to do. The contrast with China's energetic engagement with the region is stark. It suggests that the Americans understand just how weak their position is in the diplomatic dimension of their contest with China. Only Japan and Australia really seem to be rallying to America's side diplomatically.

But in the end the diplomatic dimension does not count for much one way or the other. It is comforting for Washington to imagine that the competition with China will be conducted as a kind of diplomatic and ideological beauty contest in which the countries of East Asia decide which of the rivals they prefer to see as the regional hegemon. If it was like that, then America would surely win. But that is not the way this contest will go, because the stakes are so high – especially for China. It is wrong and simplistic to say that rivalry between a rising power and an established power inevitably leads to war. But it is certainly true that the issues between America and China are exactly the kind that have driven major powers to war with one another throughout history. The possibility that their contest could lead to war is already obvious to everyone, and both sides are explicitly threatening war if the other makes a wrong move. Once war is a clear possibility, whether it actually breaks out or not, every other dimension of the contest is pushed aside. That has already happened in the US–China contest. War is not inevitable, but a test of nerves and resolve is inevitable and is already underway. It will now be decided by the balance of military power and resolve – by which of them backs off from a military confrontation, or which of them prevails if war comes because neither one backs off. The vital question – vital especially for Australia – is which side is best placed to face this test and win in it.

To understand this, we need to take a moment to step back and look at how such contests work. The essential lineaments of any regional or global order are ultimately determined by the issues over which the strongest powers – the great powers – are willing to go to war. Or rather, because perceptions count for a lot, the issues over which they can *convince* one another, and the lesser states in the system, that they are willing to go to war. So, for example, the stable European order of the nineteenth century was founded on the clear willingness of all the great powers to go to war to resist an attempt by any of them to seek hegemony. The Cold War order was defined by the evident determination of both superpowers to go to war to prevent even minor incursions into their established spheres of influence by the other. And the key to the East Asian order from 1972 until about a decade ago was the willingness of America to go to war to preserve its position as the leading regional power, and the unwillingness of any other regional power to risk war to challenge it.

By the same token, the way to change an international order is to change perceptions about the great powers' willingness to go to war. That is what China is trying to do in East Asia today. It aims to assert its place as the region's primary power, and undermine America's position, by showing that it is willing to go to war to push America out of East Asia and that America is not willing to go to war to stop it. America, if it is to resist China's challenge, must do the opposite. It must show that it is willing to fight China to preserve its position in East Asia. If it fails to do that, US allies will lose confidence in its commitments to them, the alliances will crumble and America's strategic position in Asia will collapse.

The preliminary skirmishes in this contest have been taking place over the past decade in the South and East China seas. In the South China Sea, for example, China has been deliberately testing Washington's willingness to risk a war with China by seizing contested features and building military bases. America has loudly criticised these actions, but has not done anything serious to stop them, because that would risk an armed clash that might escalate into a full-scale war. That is a risk that Washington has not been willing to take, so China has won that round. Now the contest seems to have moved on to Taiwan, where the stakes are far, far higher. The strategic future of Asia will probably be determined by whether Beijing decides to put America's resolve to the ultimate test over Taiwan.

Why would China risk it? It is sometimes argued that the strategic rivalry in Asia is more stable and manageable than it appears, drawing an analogy with the US–Soviet rivalry of the Cold War. That often looked very perilous and unstable, but the two sides avoided outright confrontation and war for forty years. Could the US–China contest work out the same way? Alas, there are good reasons to doubt that it will, because today's US–China rivalry is very different from the Cold War in some important ways. In the Cold War, both sides sought essentially to preserve the balance that emerged at the end of World War II. That balance accorded the two rivals equal status as global superpowers, each with a clearly defined sphere of influence which the other was – almost always – careful to respect. That made both sides inherently conservative. Both accepted that they could not erode the other's position and they sought mostly to ensure that they preserved their own.

The US–China contest has a quite different dynamic, because the rivals' objectives are asymmetrical. America does not see China as a great power, and does not concede to it a sphere of influence. Instead, America claims a sphere of influence over China's entire region. This is what China wants to overturn, to be replaced by an order in which China, like America, dominates its own region and is America's equal globally. To Beijing, this seems only natural now that China has drawn level with or overtaken America on so many dimensions of national power. Indeed, in most ways it is far more powerful relative to America than the Soviet Union ever was. That means China has far stronger motives to overturn the current order than either the Soviets or the United States did in the Cold War, which makes it more likely to risk a confrontation than the Cold War rivals were. Unless America starts to pull back of its own accord, China is very likely sooner or later to bring the issue to a head.

It is a test that Washington would prefer to avoid. Biden and his team often speak of their desire to manage the competition with China to avoid dangerous confrontations. He has told Xi Jinping that he wants "common-sense guardrails to ensure that competition does not veer into conflict." But that is not what Xi wants, because he aims to use the risk of conflict to show that China's power and resolve now exceeds America's. Biden's desire to avoid such risks will encourage Xi to think he can succeed. Of course Xi does not want a war with America, any more than Biden wants a war with China. Xi hopes to demonstrate, and compel Washington to acknowledge, that China has taken America's place as the leading power in Asia by making America back off to avoid a war. And of course Washington hopes that if a confrontation cannot be avoided, then it can make China back off, thus re-establishing America's primacy.

Naturally, US policy-makers would prefer that America could help Taiwan defeat a Chinese attack on its own, without having to fighting China itself. But it is a vain hope. The hard reality is that Taiwan does not take its own defence very seriously. It spends only about 2 per cent of GDP on defence – the same as Australia – which is extraordinary considering the looming threat it faces. But in truth that probably makes little difference. China's huge preponderance in power, its close proximity and its clear resolve mean that no matter how big its defence budget or how wisely it is spent, Taiwan cannot realistically expect to defend itself from China. And as we will see, the example of Ukraine doesn't change that.

Either side could easily bring on a crisis over Taiwan at any time, but Beijing is far more likely to do so than Washington. China's leaders have many reasons to act, despite all the obvious risks. Reclaiming Taiwan is a treasured goal in itself, but the opportunity to push America out of Asia and reclaim China's place at the apex of the regional order is more alluring still. Whether it is alluring enough to tempt Xi to move militarily against Taiwan will depend primarily on his assessment of Washington's response.

The more confident he is that Washington would not fight, the more likely he is to take the plunge. A great deal therefore hinges on the Chinese leadership's assessment of US resolve. Many factors will affect that assessment. On one side are the fatal consequences for America's position in Asia if it decides not to fight, and Washington's repeated declarations that it is determined to stay in Asia. But a lot of issues weigh on the other side of the scale.

One is the fact – critical in Chinese eyes – that America and its allies already acknowledge, even if they do not formally accept, China's claim to sovereignty over Taiwan. That means that – unlike Russia's invasion of Ukraine – a Chinese attack on Taiwan could not be presented as aggression by one sovereign state against another. Not just in Beijing's eyes, but in international law, Washington has already gone a long way towards accepting that what happens between Beijing and Taiwan is an internal Chinese affair, and none of America's business.

Another factor is the long-standing and very deliberate ambiguity in America's strategic commitment to Taiwan. For decades Washington has made a point of not saying whether it would send US forces into combat to resist a Chinese attack. That once made sense to discourage Taiwan from provoking a crisis, but that is no longer a danger and influential voices in Washington have argued that "strategic ambiguity" should be dropped in favour of a clear commitment. Nonetheless, it has been maintained and reaffirmed by the Biden administration. That must make Beijing more confident that America would not fight. And they are unlikely to be worried much by Biden's habit of going off-script on this question. Each time he seems to say unambiguously that America would fight for Taiwan – he's done it three times at last count – his officials swiftly and categorically correct him, which he meekly accepts. The Chinese are more likely to see these strange episodes as signs of Biden's growing incapacity rather than of stiffening US resolve.

The strongest reason for China's leaders to think that America will not fight for Taiwan is simply that it would plunge America into the biggest war since 1945, which it cannot expect to win and which might well become a nuclear war – World War III, in fact. Here we come to the heart of the whole question of America's future in Asia, and the wisdom of Australia's dependence upon it. If America cannot credibly expect to win a major war with China in Asia, then it cannot reliably or for long deter China from mounting a military challenge to its leadership in Asia, most likely over Taiwan. And if it fails to deter such a challenge, then it cannot avoid a fateful choice. Either it backs down and fatally undermines its position in Asia, or it plunges into a futile and potentially catastrophic war that it will probably lose. If it finds itself facing that terrible choice, by far the most likely as well as the most prudent choice would be to decide not to fight. The alternative would be to plunge into a war so ruinous that victory, even if it could be attained, would be meaningless. In Churchill's mordant phrase, "Victory would be bought so dear as to be almost indistinguishable from defeat."

This judgment will still surprise many people. The myth that America is militarily invincible has an astonishingly tenacious grip, even on the minds of experts who should know better, and especially in Washington and Canberra. The myth took hold thirty years ago, after the triumph of Operation Desert Storm in 1991, and has proved impervious to the succession of defeats and failures since then. But it is an illusion, even in Asia, where America's maritime supremacy has been so clear and complete for so long. Predicting the outcome of any war is a risky business, as Moscow now understands, but the factors that make a war with China over Taiwan hard for America to win are very clear. It is impossible to win a war over Taiwan without winning the battle for control of the air and sea around Taiwan itself. America has no clear way to do this, because China has decisive advantages. It is fighting close to its home bases, while America has to fight from distant bases or from very vulnerable ships. Many studies over many years confirm that as China's air and naval forces have grown, they have become increasingly able to exploit these advantages to win this battle, and then fight America to a standstill in the wider regional war that would almost certainly follow. It makes no material difference to this outcome whether US allies in the region such as Japan and Australia join the fight or not, and it is far from certain that they would.

Some people in Washington and elsewhere predict that America can win back maritime ascendancy with innovative new technologies and operational concepts. That is possible, but it will not happen quickly, and it may not happen at all because the fundamentals of the situation – strategic, geographic, technological and operational – all lean China's way. As a result, Elbridge Colby, in the best recent study of US military strategy against China, concludes that the only way America can expect to win a conventional war would be if China voluntarily agreed to keep the war limited. But there is absolutely no reason to expect the Chinese to do that. Why would they deliberately constrain themselves in ways which plainly give America an advantage? On the contrary, China has every reason to escalate a war with America precisely because – as Colby implicitly acknowledges – that is the path to victory. And once the war was underway, strategic calculation would be reinforced by emotion. Even in a limited war over Taiwan, America would have to attack military bases on Chinese territory, and China would feel compelled to retaliate against US bases in the region, including Guam. America, too, would find it hard to keep the war limited once China begin sinking major US naval ships such as aircraft carriers. This all makes it very likely that any serious clash over Taiwan would soon escalate into a wider regional war which neither side could convincingly win.

The most likely outcome of the conventional phase of the war is therefore a costly stalemate in which both sides have taken heavy losses but neither side has suffered enough to force it to abandon the fight. There would then be no apparent way to break the deadlock and secure victory through further conventional operations. This is the point at which the war risks going nuclear. It is remarkable that so little attention is given to this very real possibility by America and its allies. In the Cold War, it was universally understood that any conventional war between the United States and the Soviet Union would swiftly and almost inevitably become a nuclear war. But the fact that China has nuclear weapons is largely discounted from assessments of a US–China conflict. That is a big mistake, because a conventional stalemate would leave both sides without any path to victory except through threatening or using nuclear weapons.

America's path would be through nuclear blackmail. Washington would not plan to actually use nuclear weapons. Instead, it would threaten to initiate nuclear war against China unless Beijing abandoned the fight. American military doctrine has always encompassed this move. Since early in the Cold War, it has explicitly declared a willingness to be the first to use nuclear weapons if its conventional forces looked like losing a major war. The Biden administration is set to reaffirm this "first-use" doctrine in its 2022 Nuclear Posture Review, despite Biden's own long-standing preference to abandon it. That suggests he has been convinced that America needs to keep the nuclear blackmail option open and credible. But would it work against China? That depends on whether the Chinese believe that Washington would fulfil its threat to launch a nuclear attack on China. That is far from assured, because China can threaten to retaliate with nuclear attacks on America. Beijing's nuclear arsenal is much smaller than Washington's, but it is growing fast and is already big enough to kill many hundreds of thousands, and probably millions, of Americans. The Chinese most probably believe that it is big enough to deter an American nuclear strike. If so, they will call America's bluff and ignore its nuclear threats, and Washington's blackmail gambit will fail.

But that is not quite the last word. The leaders in Washington might convince themselves that they could deter a Chinese retaliatory strike on America by threatening an even larger counter-retaliatory attack on China. But then the Chinese might threaten counter-counter-retaliation ... and so on, perhaps ad infinitum. No one can be sure how this nightmare nuclear pas de deux, once begun, would end. But in a game of bluff like this, one thing is plain. The side with a lesser stake in the final outcome has a big disadvantage, because both sides will know that it will probably blink first. We saw this in the Cuban Missile Crisis. Khrushchev blinked when he realised that Kennedy had much more at stake over the question of Soviet nuclear missiles in Cuba than he did, and was thus less likely to back off.

Khrushchev then understood that he had better give way if he didn't want to fight a nuclear war. In a Taiwan crisis, both sides would know that the larger stake is China's, so the balance of resolve falls in its favour. America would therefore probably blink first. It is hard to imagine any US president being willing to fight a nuclear war – risking direct nuclear attack on US cities – for the sake of Taiwan, not even to preserve US leadership in Asia. The stakes for America are just not that high, as we have seen. That means a US threat to start a nuclear war would not be credible, so Washington cannot rely on nuclear blackmail to achieve the defeat of China that its conventional forces can no longer deliver. And it means that America has no clear and plausible path to victory in a war over Taiwan.

China, too, might use nuclear weapons to break a conventional stale-mate, but unlike America, its options involve actually launching a nuclear attack. It is a concept that the Russians call "escalate to de-escalate," which has been highlighted by the Ukraine crisis. The idea is to launch one or two nuclear weapons, with the aim of showing your adversary that you are willing to fight a larger nuclear war, and thereby convince them to back off or "de-escalate." This would only make sense if the attacking side was very confident that its opponents would not retaliate in kind because they were not willing to fight a nuclear war. It would have been crazy to try it in the Cold War, when both sides were equally willing to go nuclear to preserve the status quo. But these things are much more asymmetrical in the post–Cold War world. Russia's clearly implied threat to use nuclear weapons in this way to counter a direct NATO intervention in Ukraine cannot be dismissed as incredible because its stake in Ukraine is obviously much greater than America's.

By the same token, Chinese leaders may well think that this kind of move would work for them because their stake in Taiwan is clearly so much higher than America's. They might convince themselves that they could launch a nuclear attack on a US aircraft carrier or on the big US military base on Guam, and then deter a US nuclear retaliatory strike by threaten-ing counter-retaliation against US cities. They might be right, too. It would be appallingly humiliating for America to back down in the face of a Chinese nuclear strike, and many in Washington and elsewhere would say it is unthinkable. But would it not be even more unthinkable to hit back, knowing that this would almost certainly provoke devastating Chinese nuclear attacks on US cities? We'd be foolish to assume that Beijing would not be tempted to think that "escalate to de-escalate" might work for them.

There are limits to how far we can usefully go in speculating about these horrific scenarios. The reality is that no one knows what would happen once war broke out between America and China, because there has never been a major war between nuclear-armed states before. Everything we think we know about such a scenario is drawn from the lessons of the Cold War, and the US–China contest is very different in key respects. But some things are clear. One is that the clear asymmetry of resolve between America and China makes nuclear threats less useful to America than to China. The other is that on both sides decisions about nuclear war would be made under unimaginably fraught conditions. There is no reason to expect either side to act wisely or even rationally. Rage, fear, panic and exhaustion could easily swamp the calm assessment of risks and options. That should make responsible leaders very cautious indeed about allowing a crisis to escalate to war in the first place. In fact, if they understood these risks in Washington – and one can only hope they do – no moderately rational president could seriously consider going to war against China to defend America's position in Asia, when America's own direct security is not at stake.

This all has profound implications: US deterrence of China is much weaker than many in Washington or Canberra seem to realise. The Chinese know that America has no clear way to win a war, and they will probably find it hard to believe that US leaders would start a war that they too must know they cannot win. This makes it more likely that Beijing will roll the dice on Taiwan and confront America with an appalling choice. Either it steps back and abandons Taiwan, fatally weakening its entire position in Asia, or it starts a war it has no clear way of winning, with a very real risk of going nuclear. But America cannot save Taiwan or its position in Asia by fighting that war. So, either way, whether it fights or not, America's leadership in Asia would be finished.

But is that right? Might America abandon Taiwan and still preserve a strong position in Asia? That depends on the attitudes of America's Asian allies, which are vital to sustaining that position – especially Japan. That alliance will wither if Japan loses faith in Washington's commitment to defend it. Japan would then have no reason to bear the burdens of the alliance, and would start instead to make its own settlement with China. Some might argue that a Chinese move against Taiwan would make Tokyo keener than ever to cling to Washington, but the opposite is more likely. If America fails to defend Taiwan, it will raise deep and justified doubts about its willingness to defend Japan. It is not just a question of US credibility, but the more fundamental question of US imperatives and capability. If Washington had decided that Taiwan was not important enough to fight the kind of war it would have to fight against China to defend it, how sure could Tokyo be that it would not decide the same about Japan? And if America could not win a war to defend Taiwan, how sure could Tokyo be that it could win a war to defend Japan?

To reassure Japan about these questions after failing to defend Taiwan, Washington would have to do two things. The first would be to present – to the Japanese, to the Chinese and most importantly to its own people – a compelling argument as to why Japan's security mattered enough to America to justify fighting a nuclear war to defend it. As I explained earlier, that would be a hard argument to make, especially to sceptical Americans, once one got past the boilerplate rhetoric about long-standing allies and tried to explain precisely why Japan's security was worth the sacrifice of US cities – especially when Japan could easily defend itself if it chose. Second, America would need to make a truly massive investment over decades to build and sustain the forces required to win a conventional war with China. Are Americans really up for that?

Taiwan is such an important test of America's position in Asia because a crisis there would compel both Washington and its allies to confront the harsh facts which so far they have gone out of their way to ignore. They are the likelihood that China will seek to mount a military challenge to America in Asia eventually, the enormous costs and risks that America would have to accept to reliably deter such a challenge, the appalling risks that it would have to bear to fight China in Asia, the very slender chances that it could win and the lack of any truly compelling reason why it needs to try.

Perhaps something of the reality is already beginning to dawn on Washington, where there are signs that the Biden administration is toning down its rhetoric on China. At first it seemed the Biden team were determined to show that they were as tough as the Trump administration, or even tougher. But the vitriolic tone of their first meeting with their Chinese counterparts in Anchorage in March 2012 had given way by the end of the year to the much more measured tone of Biden's virtual meeting with Xi in November. That may reflect their growing realisation that an all-out strategic contest with China is going to be much harder, more costly and more dangerous than they first imagined. The impression that they are softening their line is reinforced by the modest tone and low profile of the administration's Indo-Pacific Strategy. But more striking still is the failure of the administration and its predecessors to take the steps which are so obviously essential to give themselves a chance to win this contest. It is now over a decade since Barack Obama's "Pivot to Asia," which achieved nothing. It is nearly five years since Trump's 2017 National Security Strategy declared China to be a major strategic rival, and the most Washington has done – by its own admission – is to hold meetings of the Quad and launch AUKUS.

These measures count for absurdly little compared to the scale of the task. Consider what Washington did when America entered the Cold War with the launch of the Truman Doctrine in 1947. In the following four years it established NATO and its network of alliances in Asia, launched a major program to develop its nuclear capability, deployed massive forces to Europe and Asia, and fought the Korean War. Through the 1960s, it was spending between 8 and 9 per cent of GDP on defence. In the 1980s it spent over 6 per cent, and even in 2010 it was spending almost 5 per cent. Today it spends just 3.7 per cent. Whatever its leaders might say, this is not a country that is behaving as if it is girding itself for what Biden had called "the contest for the twenty-first century."

It is perhaps too early to say that America has already begun to step back from the contest with China in Asia, but it is certainly true that it has not yet stepped up to it. So the question naturally arises: when will they start getting serious about it? Getting serious means defining a clear objective in the contest with China, developing a concrete and credible plan to achieve it and committing the resources needed to deliver it. There will be economic and diplomatic dimensions to that, but above all America must step up to the military challenges that we have highlighted. Until this changes, China will not take America's threats seriously, and it will be very hard to deter. And by the same token, it will be unwise for Australia to take America's promises seriously until we see US leaders articulating a real, concrete, credible strategy to contain China and explaining the costs and risks involved, and then see American voters accept and support the strategy despite those costs and risks.

Unless and until we see this, the question will remain open: are they serious in Washington, or are they kidding themselves? And are they kidding us? Our friends there urge us to stick with them in the contest with China, but how sure can we be that they will stick with us? Because we must never forget that America has alternatives. If China can take America's place in East Asia without being able to threaten America's overall security, then there is no vital need for America to stay in Asia at all. The twenty-first century's new and more even global distribution of power is more like the situation that America faced in the nineteenth century than throughout the twentieth century. It means America need no longer fear a Eurasian hegemon, and can therefore afford to return to the posture that served it so well for so long – the posture of avoiding strategic commitments beyond the Western hemisphere which goes by the name "isolationism."

That has implications beyond East Asia. We have already seen Washington accept that its influence has waned in the Middle East. We may well be seeing the same in Europe over the next few years, as Washington faces a choice about whether to allow the Europeans themselves to shoulder the new and heavier burden of securing Europe's eastern frontier against Russia. "Isolationism" got a bad name in the twentieth century, but it is coming back because it makes good strategic sense for America in the twenty-first century. The habit-bound experts in Washington may not see this, but US voters seem to get it. How else are we to understand the electoral success of Trump's "America First" and Biden's "A Foreign Policy for the Middle Class"? Old habits die hard, and so do old dreams, so we can expect to hear Washington policy types talking about US leadership globally and in Asia for some time to come, but the reality reflected by these new slogans is already nudging the old ones aside.

It boils down to this. In the decades ahead, China will have more power than America, especially in Asia, and it has more at stake than America too. How then can America expect to win the contest for East Asia? Why should it even try, in a world where nuclear weapons make such contests so dangerous? So the key choice we face is not whether we should abandon America, but whether we should trust them not to abandon Asia, and abandon us.

All these questions have been sharpened by Russia's invasion of Ukraine. The crisis has big implications far beyond Europe, and highlights both the issues at stake and the dangers that loom here in Asia. It also provides a tragic and important lesson in the workings of power politics – lessons which have been forgotten in recent decades. Russia's invasion is not just the most serious challenge to international order since the end of the Cold War. It is arguably the most direct and dangerous challenge to America's place in the global order since 1945. This is the first time since then that a major power – a nuclear-armed power – has used force on such a scale to challenge Washington's claims to global influence. It is a chilling demonstration of the way that power politics still works today, and of the central role that the threat and use of armed force continue to play in disputes between major powers over their roles and the reach of their influence in the international system.

The underlying issues at stake in Ukraine today are very similar to those in the contest between America and China in East Asia. Just as China wants to restore its place as a great power and as the primary power in East Asia, Russia wants to reassert its place as a great power in Eastern Europe. Like China, Russia wants a sphere of influence over its close neighbours from which other great powers are excluded, and it wants an equal place with other great powers in a multilateral global order. And, like China, these ambitions go very deep. The resolve not just of Russia's leaders but of its people to reclaim its position as a great power after a period of weakness and humiliation is not to be underestimated. It is a much bigger issue than the preservation of the current regime in the Kremlin. Many Russians who would gladly see Putin deposed nonetheless fervently believe that Russia is, and must be treated as, a great power.

Russia's opposition to the post–Cold War order reflects the failure of those who designed and built that order in Europe to find a place for Russia that it was prepared to accept. That is not to blame them for Putin's crimes or in any way to reduce his and his regime's culpability. It is to recognise that a vast and historic tragedy like the Ukraine crisis has complex causes, and that it is important to understand the full range of decisions that contributed to setting the scene for the disaster. How else can we make wiser decisions in future?

So, let's be clear. Policy-makers in Washington and some capitals of Western Europe got this wrong. They expected Russia to fit into post–Cold War Europe on the same basis as other major European countries, such as Germany, France and the UK. It was assumed, too, that Russia would be willing to surrender its status as a great power and consign its security to the collective care of a united Europe under US leadership – either as a member of NATO or a close partner. That was never going to happen, if only because Russia is not just a European country. Its territory and vital interests extend to the Middle East, Central Asia and East Asia, and the unique and Eurocentric strategic outlook and perceptions of the EU and NATO could not encompass Russia's much broader concerns. But more fundamentally, Russia's scale, history and self-perception, as well as its diminished but still formidable power, made it impossible for it to submerge itself in the collective identity of united Europe. That would have been so even if Russia's political system had not taken such a sharp authoritarian turn under Putin. If Europe's other "peripheral power," the United Kingdom, has found that it could not stomach its place in that vision of Europe, how could Russia be expected to?

So a different place had to be found for Russia in the post–Cold War European order – one that Russia was willing to accept, and that meant one that accorded with Russia's image of itself as a great power. This was understood by many of those who had steered America and its allies through the Cold War. Right at the outset, Germany's leaders warned against NATO expansion into Eastern Europe, and in 1998, as the first new members were admitted, George Kennan criticised it as "a tragic mistake" and "the beginning of a new Cold War." Those who have more recently been so determined to keep the door open for Ukraine to join NATO cannot claim to be surprised that Moscow has drawn the line there. Nor can they claim that there is something inherently wrong with Moscow's claim to exclude other powers from its "near abroad," because America, Australia and many other countries do the same. Washington claims and enforces an exclusive sphere of influence over the entire Western hemisphere, and Canberra's reaction to the China–Solomon Islands security agreement reminds us how jealously we attempt to guard the sphere of influence we claim in the Southwest Pacific.

But while it would be hypocritical to criticise Moscow's aim to maintain a sphere of influence over its closer neighbours, it is legitimate to condemn what it has done to try to achieve it, for two reasons. There can be no justification for invading a sovereign state and trying to erase its independent identity, as Moscow is attempting to do. That goes way beyond what is required or can be justified to assert a sphere of influence. And there can be no justification under any circumstances for the extraordinary brutality of Russia's military operations in Ukraine, especially the widespread and systematic targeting of civilians.

Nonetheless, we should be careful where justified outrage at Russia's conduct might lead us. The worse Russia behaves, and more bewilderingly brutal and incompetent its military appears, the more obvious it seems that the only acceptable endpoint for the crisis is Russia's total defeat and humiliation. The temptation is to keep expanding support for Ukraine and punishment of Russia to the point that Russia is forced to capitulate, and the poor performance of Russia's armed forces might make this seem easy. So why not, for example, keep pushing until Russian forces are expelled from all Ukrainian territory, including Crimea, and then bring Ukraine into the EU, severely restrict Russia's commercial and economic connections with Europe, allow Sweden and Finland into NATO, and perhaps even bring Ukraine into NATO too? The temptation is clearly there. In late April, the US Secretary of Defense, Lloyd Austin, said, "We want to see Russia weakened to the degree that it can't do the kinds of things that it has done in invading Ukraine."

Such ambitious aims would be misguided, for three reasons. The first is the danger of escalation. The harder Russia is pushed, the more likely it is to lash out against Ukraine's supporters, especially America. It has plenty of opportunities to do so. For example, America is reportedly giving Ukrainian forces a great deal of detailed real-time operational intelligence, which has contributed a lot to its successes against Russian forces. Much of that information will have come from US satellites, which Moscow has the capacity to attack with anti-satellite weapons. Putin might well decide that this would be an effective way of hitting back at Washington, and it would leave Biden with difficult decisions about how to respond. More worrying still is the possibility that Putin might decide to attack the supply chains supporting Ukrainian forces in neighbouring countries such as Poland. This would leave Washington and its allies with a very difficult choice indeed between backing off or retaliating. Retaliation would lead to the kind of direct NATO–Russia clashes which Biden and others have been so determined to avoid, because they raise the risk of a nuclear exchange.

The possibility that Moscow might use nuclear weapons cannot be entirely dismissed. As we saw in exploring China's nuclear options, the uncertainty of US resolve raises the possibility that "escalating to de-escalate" could work. Putin might convince himself that he could use a nuclear weapon against Ukraine and deter any US nuclear retaliation by threatening counter-retaliation against America itself. Biden's determination to avoid what he called "World War III" by keeping US and NATO forces out of the fight in Ukraine could encourage Putin to think that Washington would step back from a nuclear exchange. Of course, even without a US nuclear response, the consequences for Russia of using nuclear weapons would be appalling, but the worse things get for Russia, the less it might seem Putin has to lose. This danger must be considered as the West weighs the endgame in Ukraine.

The second reason for the West to keep its aims in the Ukraine crisis modest is the need to find a place for Russia in a stable and sustainable European order. Whatever happens, Russia will not go away, and the rest of Europe must learn to live with it if it is to have a peaceful future. History plainly shows that the way to win the peace is to offer adversaries a respectable place in the international system with which they can be satisfied. That is how peace was built after the Napoleonic Wars, when France was brought into the Concert of Europe, and after World War II, when Germany and Japan were successfully integrated into the post-war order. By contrast, this is what didn't happen in 1919, when Germany was locked out of the post-war system in Europe, and again with Russia after 1991. The alternative to a settlement which Russia can live with is a state of permanent hostility with a still-formidable adversary armed with nuclear weapons. That would be bad for the whole of Europe, and especially for Ukraine itself, which cannot hope for a secure future unless its relationship with Russia and Russia's position in Europe are established on a sustainable basis acceptable to all.

And there is one further vital consideration. As we have seen, a strong Russia is a key to managing China. In the long run, Europe and America will rely on a strong Russia that remains independent of China to ensure that China cannot move on from hegemony in East Asia to dominate Eurasia and threaten Europe. We can be sure that Russia will be determined not to become a Chinese satellite, but Europe and others will depend on it having the power to do so. It will be as well to keep that in mind when thinking about Russia's future after the Ukraine crisis.

The Ukraine crisis and the question of Russia's future in Europe therefore pose the same quintessential challenge of order-building as Asia faces in dealing with China. How do we balance the principles and ideals on which we believe international relations should be based on the one hand, with the need to maintain peace and stability on the other? That calls for difficult compromises in a world where there are powerful states whose principles and ideals do not accord with ours. There are profound moral imperatives on both sides of the balance, as we weigh the values embodied by those principles and ideals against the imperative to avoid war, especially nuclear war. Peace is a value too.

This is what "realism" in international affairs, properly so called, is all about. The cold calculus of national interests, and the distribution of power, especially military power, are not the only things that matter. But they do matter, and disaster follows when they are overlooked. This was the reality that Roosevelt and Churchill faced when they met Stalin at Yalta in Crimea in the last months of World War II to frame the post-war international order. They confronted a choice between conceding Stalin's demand for an exclusive sphere of influence over Eastern Europe or fighting a new war against an adversary even more formidable than the Third Reich. Their choice, which many have since condemned as a betrayal, left half of Europe under Soviet domination for forty-five years and caused great suffering. But it prevented a war which they judged would have been far worse – and who can say they were wrong? Of course, Russia today is not the Soviet Union of 1945, its humiliated army is certainly not the Red Army that outfought the Wehrmacht all the way to Berlin, and Putin is but a pallid imitation of Stalin as a practitioner of power politics. But the task that leaders in Europe and America today face in negotiating the endgame of the Ukraine crisis is in essence somewhat similar. Thirty years after the end of the Cold War, Europe needs "a new Yalta" to agree the terms of Russia's place in Europe and relations with America in the post-Soviet era, just as in East Asia we need to agree new terms for China's place in the region and its relations with America in the era of Chinese power.

The specific challenges of creating a new order in Europe are different from those in East Asia, because the distribution of power is different. China is much stronger than Russia, both in itself and relative to its regional neighbours, and its ambitions are bigger. Russia today is not the Soviet Union of 1945, and Europe today is unrecognisably different. Russia cannot dominate Europe, and it cannot compel change to the foundations of today's European order. But its concerns about how the working of that order affects what it sees as its vital interests cannot be ignored and must to some degree be accommodated, and that will require some adjustments to the way the European order works where it intersects with Russia's direct interests. Exactly how that can be done, what should be conceded to Moscow and what should be refused, is too big a subject to explore here.

But however the current crisis ends, a much larger effort will be required to defend NATO's eastern frontier in the years ahead than anything seen or contemplated so far. It is only prudent to expect that Russia's military will learn and recover from its failures in Ukraine and restore some of the qualities it has so often shown in the past. Major forces from NATO's strongest members will need to be permanently forward-deployed in the weaker front-line states, requiring considerable sustained increases in defence budgets and force numbers, perhaps requiring for some countries a return to compulsory military service.

All this has significant implications for America's future strategic commitments. Will America continue to play the leading role in European security that it has accepted since the end of the Cold War, as the costs and risks increase? As we have seen, America's imperatives to defend Europe are much weaker than they were, and Europe itself is much stronger and more able to defend itself. So it makes less and less sense for America to shoulder the burdens of European security the way it has since the Cold War ended. The higher the costs of doing so, the sooner the pressure to shed this unnecessary – and increasingly onerous and dangerous – burden will overcome the sentimental attachments and policy inertia which have sustained the commitment for so long after its original rationale evaporated. Then Europe itself will have to shoulder that burden, which it is perfectly able to do.

What does this mean for America's position globally? Does it enhance US leadership in Asia and make it more able to resist China's challenge? Some argue that America's position has been strengthened because the response to Russia's invasion will have made Beijing more cautious about moving against Taiwan. There may be some truth in this. Beijing will certainly have taken note of the nature and scale of the economic sanctions imposed on Russia and be taking steps to minimise its vulnerabilities to such measures. But China's economy is bigger and more robust than Russia's, and much more costly for other countries to sanction. It would be unwise to assume that the risk of economic sanctions would materially affect China's decisions about Taiwan one way or the other. Nor will Beijing be much swayed by Russia's failures on the battlefield. Certainly, Ukraine's successes should remind Chinese leaders not to take the outcome of any battle for granted, but the military situations are very different. In particular, it would be easy for China to control the sea off Taiwan, and thus far harder for Taiwan's friends to supply it with the weapons that have made such a difference in Ukraine. And the Chinese will no doubt expect their forces to perform much better than Russia's – as indeed they might.

So the more important implications of the Ukraine crisis in Asia relate to America's position rather than China's. Since the Ukraine crisis broke, there has been much talk that American global leadership has been revived and its credibility restored by its success in orchestrating a broad international response to Russia's aggression. This is premature. It is far from clear that Washington has any coherent idea of what it is trying to achieve in Ukraine or how to achieve it. There is plenty of scope yet for things to go badly wrong. Moreover, the international response to America's lead in the crisis has been far from encouraging. No one is surprised that China has refused to follow Washington's lead, but it is striking that so many other countries, including many democracies, have sat on the fence. They include India and Indonesia, Brazil and Mexico, and South Africa. Even in Europe, there has been a lot of dissent on Russia, reflecting among other things the deeper understanding in Berlin and Paris than in Washington that Europe has no choice but to find a way to live with Russia.

More specifically, does it strengthen US deterrence of China over Taiwan? It is hard to argue that it does. All the tough talk since the invasion began cannot detract from the fact that since early in the crisis the Biden administration has consistently and very clearly ruled out sending US forces to defend Ukraine. This, even though Russia's threat to Ukraine was clearly understood as a very serious threat to the US-led post–Cold War order in Europe and globally. There is no question that Biden is right not to fight for Ukraine. But Biden did not need to rule out US military intervention so clearly, and it is possible that he might have prevented the invasion, or limited its scope, had he left things a little more open. The fact that he closed off the military option the way he did suggests two things. First, that he did not think the American people would be willing to contemplate war with Russia over Ukraine. Second, that Biden did not think Putin would take the possibility of US military intervention seriously, so there was a grave danger that his bluff would be called. This tells us that Biden believes Americans were not willing to fight a nuclear-armed power, even over an issue vital to preserving US global leadership – and that America's rivals know that. And that implies that Biden at some level understands that America does not have the power and resolve to defend the global role it lays claim to.

Of course, this has big implications for Taiwan, and for America's position in Asia. It is hard to argue that America is more strongly committed to Taiwan's defence than to Ukraine's. On the contrary, while it does not have full-scale treaty commitments to either of them, Washington made less formal but still very significant written undertakings to protect Ukraine's security under the Budapest Memorandum of 1994. And the fact it had been so eager to give Kyiv a path to NATO membership surely implied that Washington saw Ukraine's defence as a vital US interest it was willing to defend by force.

None of that is true of Taiwan. America has no commitments to defend Taiwan. The *Taiwan Relations Act* only requires the president to help Taiwan defend itself, not to send US forces to defend it directly. On the contrary, under its policy of strategic ambiguity Washington has explicitly refused to make any commitment. Most significant of all, perhaps, America recognises Ukraine as a sovereign state and a member of the United Nations, which entails obligations to support and help defend its independence and integrity. By contrast, America does not recognise Taiwan as a sovereign state. So why should anyone expect it to defend Taiwan from China when it was not willing to defend Ukraine from Russia? And how can America preserve its position in Asia if it is not willing to defend Taiwan? That seems likely to be one key lesson of the Ukraine crisis for Asia. The other is a warning not to try to perpetuate an international order which leaves major powers dissatisfied, because that raises the risks of war. The way to survive and prosper in times of rapid strategic change is not to cling to an old and unsustainable vision of order which is out of step with the new distribution of power, but to help build a new one that matches the new realities better, with all the difficult compromises that must entail.

Professor Kerry Brown is a renowned China scholar at King's College London. In an earlier life he was a UK diplomat in Beijing, where he served in the boom years after China joined the World Trade Organization in 2001. He wrote a short and pungent book that drew on this experience, reflecting on diplomats and diplomacy. He recounts how little his colleagues in Beijing at the time understood of the astonishing economic and strategic transformation happening right in front of them as China's economy quadrupled in size in ten years. He has written more recently that "this was not because we weren't perfectly capable of seeing the change – but because we didn't want to." Diplomats "were the ultimate defenders of the current paradigms and resisted the idea of any new ones emerging to make their lives harder." That was because "categorical spelling out of unwelcome truths was – well, unwelcome" to their superiors back in London.

It is a pithy and precise description of a problem that afflicts public servants of all kinds, not just diplomats, and not just in Britain. It perfectly captures an important part of how Canberra has got both China and America so wrong over the past twenty years, as China's power and ambition have grown, and America has failed to respond. Of course, ministers ultimately decide while officials only advise, but the reality is more complex than that, so no history of these years and their missteps will be complete without describing what I think will be seen as a serious and systemic failure of our intelligence, defence and foreign policy establishments, and the penumbra of think-tanks and university departments that surround them, to help ministers understand what has been happening and what they should do about it. It has been so much easier for them to keep reassuring ministers that America will always be there for us than to think through what it would mean if it is not. The worse relations with China have become, the harder it has been to suggest that there is anything we can do except rely on America to protect us.

Nonetheless, these are thoughtful and intelligent people, and it is clear that many of them have doubts about where things are heading. There is an emerging but still largely unvoiced consensus in official Canberra that in the long run Australia will have to learn to live with a more powerful China, and that America will have to do the same. These people recognise that we cannot count on being able to perpetuate the old US-led order that served us so well. Instead, we will see a new regional order in which China has more power and America has less. They speak vaguely but confidently of a new multipolar order in the wider Indo-Pacific region in which America plays a smaller but still important role to limit China's influence and help shield us from its pressure. They expect India, too, will help balance China and keep its hegemonic impulses in check, and Japan to play its part as well.

But, like those people in Washington who accept that US primacy in Asia cannot be sustained, their counterparts in Canberra have no clear idea of how this order would work, nor of how it could be built and sustained. They assume that India will interest itself deeply in strategic affairs throughout the Indo-Pacific, rather than focus on its own sphere in South Asia and the Indian Ocean. They assume that China can be convinced or compelled to accept a continued strong US role in East Asia. They assume that Japan will have the will and strength to stand up to China. And they assume that America will be willing to carry the burdens of this balancing role when its own vital interests do not compel it to do so.

This new regional order is an attractive possibility, and it is clear why it appeals to the official establishment in Canberra. It offers a way to reconcile the now inescapable fact of Chinese power with a continued determination to rely on others, and especially America, to shield us from it. We should not perhaps abandon hope that something like it can evolve, and we should certainly do nothing that makes it harder to achieve – an issue we will return to. But just as we cannot bet our future on US primacy, we cannot base our policy, and our whole vision of our future in Asia, on the hope that the old US-led Asia-Pacific order will be replaced by a benign, multipolar Indo-Pacific order.

In fact, the odds are heavily against it. Instead, the most likely outcome over the next couple of decades is that the US-led era in our region will give way to an Asia divided between two regional hegemonies, one under India and the other under China. India will dominate South Asia and the Indian Ocean, and China will dominate East Asia and the Western Pacific. Each of them will be strong enough to deter the other from seriously interfering in its sphere of influence, but they will naturally push and shove one another along the boundary between their spheres, which will run from Myanmar and Thailand down through Malaysia, Indonesia, Australia and New Zealand.

The division of Asia into spheres of influence in this way would accord with strategic trends around the world as the US-led post–Cold War order fades. We should thus expect to see a multipolar global order in which a number of great powers, each with its own sphere of influence, compete and cooperate. Some parts of this geopolitical jigsaw are easy to foresee: America in the Western Hemisphere, Europe under some version of the EU, Russia with what it calls its "near abroad," China in East Asia and India in South Asia. Others are harder: the Middle East under Iran, perhaps, or Turkey? And what of Africa?

It is easy to see how this new order will work at the global level. It will resemble the old multipolar order of great powers in Europe for four centuries before 1914. None of the regional great powers will be strong enough to dominate the others. Their relationships will be inherently competitive, but the competition will be moderated by a classic "balance of power" regime. This would generally ensure that any aspiring global hegemon would be blocked by a formidable coalition of other great powers – peacefully where possible, by war if necessary. The dangers of war in the nuclear age might help them to reach more or less explicit understandings to avoid or limit conflict, the way Europe's "concert of powers" did between 1815 and 1914. Either way, they would have to deal flexibly with one another to manage global questions, while competing with the neighbouring great powers along the boundaries of their spheres of interest.

One thing is clear. If or when America does step back from Asia, it is hard to see what could stop China dominating East Asia and the Western

Pacific. No other country in the region has either the power or the disposition to resist it. Today, Japan is the only other potential great power in the region, and the one that seems most likely to resist Chinese hegemony. But it is already far weaker than China, and will become weaker still in the years ahead. Recent estimates from the Department of Foreign Affairs and Trade suggest that by 2035 Japan's GDP will be just one-eighth the size of China's. It will still be a prosperous and formidable country, but it will be no match for China in raw power. Nor, it seems, will it match China in resolve, if the evidence of the past decade or two is any guide.

Japan's leaders have been acutely conscious of China's growing strength and ambition for a long time now and have become more and more anxious about it. Much fuss has been made of Tokyo's moves to build up its strategic weight in response. But it is surprising how little this amounts to: Japan's defence spending is still only about 1 per cent of GDP. It still fiercely debates the legitimacy of military operations that other countries regard as routine. Its leaders still fret endlessly about how far they can go to fight alongside allies. And they have still not freed themselves of their absurd constitutional prohibition on armed forces. For all the tough talk from some quarters in Tokyo, very little has really changed in Japan as China's threat has grown. That must make us wonder whether it ever will, so it is hard to see Japan stepping up as a great power in Asia, or even as a major ally of the United States, in the years ahead. The most we can expect is that as US power fades, Japan will build armed forces, including nuclear forces, strong enough to defend itself from China and preserve a degree of independence as a strong middle power within China's sphere of influence.

The other potential major power in East Asia is Indonesia. By 2035 its economy will be as big as Japan's, and on credible estimates it will be the fourth-largest in the world before mid-century. But it will still be far smaller than China's, and it is far from clear that Jakarta can successfully channel Indonesia's potential strengths into effective international power – or how hard it will try to do so. It will not stop China dominating East Asia. The most we can expect is that it might emerge as a strong middle power, like Japan. But its size and position on the boundary between India's sphere of influence and China's will make it a significant factor in both spheres. It will have great opportunities to play the two regional hegemons off against one another to maximise its independence from both, which is what buffer states between great powers so often do.

How Indonesia plays that game, and how effectively it plays it, will be important to Australia. We too have coastlines on both the Indian Ocean and the Western Pacific, so China and India will both look to draw us into their spheres of influence, and to keep us out of their rival's sphere. Exploiting this position may well be the key to Australia's future relations with both regional hegemons, and how much opportunity we have to do so will depend a lot on how well Indonesia exploits its position. Plus, of course, there is the question of our own bilateral relations with Indonesia. It cannot compete on equal terms with India and China, but it may well be a great power in our nearer region. It will be a much greater influence on Australia, for good or ill, than it has ever been before.

This is the world and the region in which Australia must survive and flourish in the decades ahead. How well do our present policies measure up to that task?

Relations with China

Most obviously, Canberra's complete alignment with Washington in the new Cold War has made it harder to manage our relations with China. Naturally we blame China for things having gone so badly. But if we step back from the illusion that America can make our China problem go away, it must be clear that we need to find a way to live and work with the China of today. The Morrison government repeatedly claimed that it would be impossible for Australia to explore how that could be done without surrendering our sovereignty. As if give and take, compromise and adjustment are not the essence of relations between sovereign states, just as they are between people. Under Scott Morrison, Australia's position was that the only acceptable basis of a future Australia–China relationship is for China to accept our version – which is Washington's version – of the future regional order and China's place in it. China will not accept that, and America cannot force it to, and neither of course can we. Somehow we need to move past the rupture in relations with Beijing over the past four years to build the relationship we are going to need with China over the years to come. That does not mean surrendering to whatever Beijing demands, allowing China to dictate the terms of the relationship, but it does mean that we cannot expect to dictate the terms of the relationship either. We need to negotiate and compromise to defend our own interests in building a workable relationship with a very important country. Our fixation with Washington means we have missed opportunities to do this.

Relations with America

As well as missing opportunities in Beijing, we are missing them in Washington. Instead of helping America to manage the strategic transition in Asia wisely, we are encouraging Washington to confront Beijing in a contest it cannot win. Our noisy advocacy for a hard line on China strengthens the voices arguing for that approach in Washington. This is absolutely against our interests, because the hardline policy is bound to fail. Given the raw facts of power and resolve, America will step back from leadership in Asia sooner or later. Our aim should therefore be to do whatever we can to help smooth the transition from the old US role in Asia to whatever follows, because our interests are served by the evolution of a new stable, harmonious US–China relationship. If there is to be any hope of America continuing to play a significant strategic role in our region as part of a new multipolar regional order, that must come through some form of US–China accommodation. The more we support the bellicose voices in Washington, the less likely that is.

We should not underestimate our influence on this issue. The inner circle of Asia policy players in Washington is surprisingly small, and often surprisingly impressionable. Australia looms quite large for them – larger than our weight and capacities warrant. One can see this in the way they so often talk up our support for their policies, and above all in the profile they have given to AUKUS, which they have oversold almost as much as we have. This means we have a voice in Washington, but we never use it except to cheer for whatever they decide to do. That should change. Ours should be the calm voice that Washington needs to hear, suggesting a realistic, achievable China policy that better serves both US interests and our own. That would do America a favour as well as us, and enhance our longer-term standing in a town where we will always be looking for friends and influence.

Instead of that, Canberra's rhetoric helps raise the risk of the worst outcome for Australia: a war between China and America, in which we are likely to be involved. Over the past decade, and without any serious discussion, Australian governments have come to believe that America should go to war with China if necessary to preserve US primacy in Asia, and that Australia should, as a matter of course, go to war with it. Peter Dutton was very frank about this. He said he wants peace, but he also said that whether war comes is "a question for the Chinese." That is the language of war advocates throughout the ages. He thinks it is entirely up to Beijing's leaders to take the steps needed to prevent war, and if they don't then we should fight. Nor was Dutton alone. His remarks, including his notorious comment that it would be "inconceivable" for Australia not to support America in a war with China, simply said out loud what many politicians and officials think. And it is not just talk. Decisions such as the AUKUS nuclear submarine deal plainly show that supporting America in a war with China is what our armed forces are being built to do.

Dutton seemed to believe that his tough talk will help deter China from pushing its ambitions. If so, he was seriously underestimating China's resolve and Australia's power. Perhaps, after all, it was just political posturing. But whether Dutton took his own talk seriously matters less than whether other people did, especially in Washington and Beijing. Canberra's escalating war talk plainly encourages Washington to expect our support if it chooses to go to war against China. We probably underestimate the effect this might have on the handful of people who are likely to be in the White House Situation Room if and when the hard choices for war or peace must be made. Canberra's eager talk of fighting China would weigh on the side of those around the table who argue for war – just as our eagerness to fight in 1914 helped push the British Cabinet's decision for war in that grim year.

Missile bases here?

Our pro-war posture will do us great damage even if it never comes to war itself. As long as America clings to the idea that it can defeat China's challenge by deterring it militarily, it will be eager to draw its eager ally more and more closely into its military plans and preparations for war with China. This brings a new dynamic to the alliance, because until now there has never been much operational substance to match the soaring political rhetoric. That is striking when compared with America's allies in NATO or elsewhere in Asia, which host US combat forces and often forward-deploy them in preparation for contingencies.

Not since the Pacific War has America operated combat forces from our territory. Even the US force deployments through Darwin in recent years have so far been training missions. Nor have Australian forces been forward-deployed for operations with US forces in Asia. In fact, Australia has not fired a shot in support of America in Asia since we came home from Vietnam. But this will change as America presses Australia to provide real support against China. Already the expansion of US training activities in Darwin and elsewhere suggests a growing operational focus, and so does the deepening of joint capability development projects, including AUKUS. The joint facility at Pine Gap will become more important in supporting US military operations in Asia. But there will be more.

The logic of US declaratory policy and the operational challenges they face strongly suggest that if they are serious about confronting China, Washington's leaders will have to look for a lot more from us in the years ahead. It is clear what that may mean. The geographical realities are that basing US conventional naval and air forces in Australia will be of little operational value in a war over Taiwan. We are just too far from the key battlefields. But we are ideally placed to host US intermediate-range missiles targeting China.

America was unable to deploy weapons of this class anywhere under a treaty signed with the Soviets in the 1980s. Washington binned that agreement in 2019, mostly so it could deploy them in East Asia to counter China's missiles. US strategists hope that US missiles based in the Western Pacific would more effectively deter a Chinese "escalate to de-escalate" strike, and that a US strike from bases in our region would be less likely to provoke a Chinese counterstrike on the continental United States than one launched from the US itself. If Washington is serious about preserving a viable US military posture in Asia, it will have to deploy such forces somehow. And while such missiles can carry conventional warheads, they only make strategic and operational sense to deliver nuclear weapons.

In 2019, Washington got a frosty reception when it asked Canberra to consider hosting these missiles. But a lot has changed since then – including AUKUS, which has been so loudly hailed in both countries as marking a much deeper and more intimate strategic relationship than ever before. It would be surprising if Washington did not, sooner or later, take advantage of AUKUS to press Canberra to rethink its earlier refusal. Basing intermediate-range missiles somewhere across the northwest of our continent would be ideal, because they would be close enough to strike China but far enough to be relatively secure from pre-emptive attack. And how could Canberra refuse without trashing the whole AUKUS concept? Nonetheless, it would be a huge step. Australia has never hosted nuclear forces on our territory before. Nor have we ever placed ourselves on the front line of US military operations against China. China would react severely, of course. That might not matter if we were sure that America would stick around to look after us. But what if it doesn't? Basing intermediate-range nuclear forces here in Australia would not fix the fundamental weakness of America's position in Asia, so it would not reduce the chances that

Washington will sooner or later withdraw from the region. Then we'd be left facing an even more vindictive China on our own.

Our problem is that steps like that – which would draw us much more deeply into an American military confrontation with China – will not increase the likelihood that America prevails, but will vastly increase the damage to our interests when it fails. It is worth taking a moment to imagine just what that might mean in practice, if and when Australia is left without US support to find our way in a Chinese-dominated East Asia. We would risk being seen by China as a "rogue state" and treated accordingly. We'd face harsher diplomatic isolation, fewer economic opportunities and more military pressure from Beijing, and less support and cooperation from our more prudent neighbours. It would make it that much harder to build the relationship with China we will need in the years ahead.

Nor is this the only way in which Australia's present course draws us more and more closely into a losing military strategy against China. The spirit of AUKUS and the logic of the Morrison government's position make it close to inevitable that Australia will be entangled in detailed US war planning for a conflict with China – if it has not happened already. This is the way America operates with other close allies around the world, such as in NATO. Now, as the prospect of war with China grows, and as Canberra so forcefully declares its willingness to fight, it would be surprising if the war planners in Washington and Hawaii were not eager to tie down in detail exactly how Australia would contribute to a US-led coalition. It is hard to imagine that the Morrison government would have refused. The danger is that once we allow US military staffs to build Australian forces into their war plans, it becomes far harder for us to make an independent decision about going to war when a crisis breaks.

Third, Australia's ever-closer embrace of US policy on China and our confidence in America's ability to manage China for us leads us to neglect and mismanage our own defence. The Morrison government made much of its record in defence, boasting of increased spending and new capabilities to meet what it kept telling us are the most demanding strategic circumstances we have faced since the 1930s. It vastly oversold its achievements.

Start with the money. Defence spending grew steadily under the Coalition, edging back above 2 per cent of GDP and heading for 2.5 per cent, according to Peter Dutton in October 2021. This would get us back to the spending levels of the 1980s. But it would leave us far below the levels of the 1950s and 1960s, let alone what it would have been prudent for us to spend in the 1930s had we seen what was coming. So there is a clear mismatch between the way Canberra talks about our strategic risks and the amount of money it is spending, and what we are getting. In fact, very little is changing for the bulk of the ADF. Only a small fraction of the $270 billion that the Coalition government claimed to be spending on new capabilities is really new. Most of it is to be spent on things that have been in the pipeline for years. The Morrison government was not wrong about the sharp rise in our strategic risks, but the scale of the response does not suggest that it took its own warnings seriously.

But just spending more money will not be enough for us to meet these risks. Everything depends on what we spend it on, and on how efficiently we spend it. Making smart decisions about that depends first on having a clear idea of what we want our forces to do. That should be obvious, but for nearly twenty years now, under both Labor and Coalition governments, our defence policy has drifted without clear strategic objectives or a military strategy to achieve them. Instead, we have childish slogans such as "Shape, Deter, Respond," which was all the Morrison government's Defence Strategic Update of 2020 had to offer in their place. This has meant that we have no basis for deciding what kinds of forces we need, so we spend a lot of money on things with no clear purpose – such as the new tanks ordered earlier this year for $3.5 billion, to take just one rather modest example.

There is no escaping the conclusion that for all the talk about national security, the Morrison government was not serious about strengthening Australia's armed forces to meet the dangers of the years and decades ahead. It is easy to see why. Like so many Australian political leaders before them, Morrison and his colleagues were content to rely on others – on our great and powerful friends – for our defence. The more they looked to America to handle our China problem, and the more they enmeshed us in Washington's military strategy, the less important it seemed to them to develop Australia's independent capability to defend ourselves and our most important interests in the more dangerous Asia of the decades ahead.

AUKUS

All this – the complacency, the incompetence, the illusions – came together in the proposal to acquire nuclear-powered submarines under AUKUS. Nothing better illustrates how badly our governments and our defence establishment are failing to meet the strategic demands of the twenty-first century, and how central to that failure is the mounting passion with which our governments cling to America. Submarines really matter to our defence, because they are the best way to deny the wider oceans that surround us and our neighbours to an adversary that wants to project power by sea against us. They become more important to us the more dangerous our strategic circumstances become, so replacing the old Collins-class boats with a new submarine force that really works for us is vital. But things started going wrong right from the start of the replacement process in the mid-2000s. Navy planners had no coherent military strategy to guide them, and thus no clear idea of what the new subs were supposed to do. So they decided to aim for the best sub they could possibly imagine – the biggest, most capable, most complex conventional submarine ever conceived – designed from scratch and built in Australia.

Not surprisingly, these wild ambitions produced a plan that was impractical, expensive and very risky. When Labor came to power in 2007, the plan presented to successive defence ministers was so scary that they sat on it, and years were wasted. When the Coalition took over in 2013, Tony Abbott decided to scrap those plans completely and buy subs from Japan instead. By the time Malcolm Turnbull was in charge, the Japan option had been scrapped and the old, wildly ambitious plans were revived. So much time had now been lost that it seemed best to rush ahead with a half-baked contest, which the French won by offering a nuclear-powered sub with the reactor replaced by diesel engines. Their bid was extremely expensive – perhaps double the price of the competitors' – very risky and was going to take so long to deliver that most if not all of the old *Collins* boats would have to be retired before their replacements could be delivered. What was worse, in the rush to get things moving, the government signed up with the French before the price, the performance and the delivery schedule had been tied down, so there was no competitive pressure on the French to perform. It was a disaster that defied every rule of project management – and one almost entirely of Australia's own making.

Right at the heart of this disaster was the assumption – seldom articulated and never seriously contested – that the key role of Australia's submarines is to join the US Navy in American operations against China in the South China Sea. From that, it followed that Australia needed a submarine that was optimised to operate at that range and which could perform as much like a US submarine as possible. And from that it was a short step to decide that what we really needed were nuclear-powered submarines. The Morrison government said that it scrapped the French project and went for nuclear-powered subs because of the rapidly deteriorating strategic situation. It claimed that China's growing threat since the French deal was signed meant we needed the additional capability that nuclear boats could provide. That doesn't hold water, because the government had been talking up our growing strategic risks long before it made the shift to AUKUS. What really drove it was the growing awareness that the French project was a debacle, and the ever-increasing desire to align ever closer with Washington. So the government opted to leap from one debacle into another, even deeper and more disastrous.

There are three broad reasons why it is a mistake for Australia to try to replace the *Collins* boats with nuclear-powered subs – or SSNs, as the Navy calls them. The first is the balance between capability, cost and numbers. SSNs have some important advantages over conventional diesel-electric boats, of which the most important is speed when submerged. They can get to a distant area of operations faster, catch their targets more easily and get out of trouble quicker. But they are, on the government's rubbery numbers, something like three times more expensive, so we could get twenty-five conventional submarines – updates of the old *Collins* design, for example – for the price of the eight SSNs the government plans to buy. The question then is whether SSNs are three times better than new conventional boats. The answer is probably no, especially if we are not fighting in the South China Sea with America, but closer to home in our own defence, where the SSNs' speed of transit makes less difference. As so often, the advantage lies with quantity over quality.

Second, building and operating SSNs involves huge technical demands and big risks. The navy must master immensely complex and critical technologies of which it knows nothing, and with no real base of national expertise to draw on. That must increase the danger that technical and safety problems will plague Australian SSNs and reduce their strategic value. It must also increase our dependence on whichever of our AUKUS partners supplies the subs, to the point that we may not be able to operate them independently at all.

And third, there is the question of timing. On the most optimistic estimates, the first SSNs might enter service in the early 2040s. But one submarine is not a serious force. We won't have an operationally viable or strategically significant submarine capability of six boats until the early 2050s at least – and given the risks and complexities involved, probably much later. Long before then, America will probably have pulled out of Asia, and it will therefore have little or no interest in supporting our SSN aspirations. And by that time, our old submarines will no longer be fit to go to sea, so we will have no submarines in service at a time of high strategic risk. We will also have lost the pool of skilled submariners needed to operate them, so we will have to rebuild our submarine force from scratch, over decades. Talk of shortening these timelines by leasing US or UK boats is fanciful – they have none to spare. So the net result of twenty years of muddle and incompetence, culminating in the folly of AUKUS, will be the collapse of our submarine force.

The obvious solution is to scrap the SSN plan or defer it indefinitely, and instead build a class of capable conventional boats modelled on the current *Collins* class – just as fast as we possibly can. This is what we will probably do, if sanity prevails.

Meanwhile, the AUKUS proposal perfectly illuminates the shallowness of the Morrison government's approach to managing our strategic risks over the decades ahead. It talked as if submarines delivered thirty years from now will help deter today's strategic challenge from China. It ignored the looming collapse of a vital capability in favour of the political and diplomatic symbolism of ever-deeper dependence on America, content in the conviction that Australia's own forces don't matter because it took for granted that we can rely on America. And, perhaps most absurdly of all, it mistook the commercial opportunism and post-Brexit geopolitical posturing that drew Britain into AUKUS for a genuine strategic commitment to Australia's security. Have we learnt nothing since 1941? In the annals of defence policy failure, it is hard to recall anything more absurd than this whole sad mess.

What of our foreign policy? Here, too, our fixation on America as the solution to our problems with China is seriously distorting our thought and action. We should be doing all we can to build the closest rapport and cooperation with our neighbours in Asia as we all try to find ways to deal with the radical shift in the regional order now underway. But instead, our diplomacy is limited to delivering Washington's talking points as our own, trying to convince our neighbours to support our dream of restored US primacy.

The problems start with our relations with the two largest powers in Asia after China. The Morrison government followed Washington in framing our relationships with India and Japan almost entirely within the "Quad." That seriously misunderstands where these two important countries are heading, and it prevents us from developing the relations with them that we will need in the new Asia.

That is especially true of India. In the decades ahead, India's power and proximity will make it very important to Australia, but not in the way we imagine now. Our Quad-centric approach sees India almost entirely as a counterweight to China and a loyal ally in the struggle to defend the US-led regional order. Scott Morrison spoke of our shared values and commitment to a liberal-democratic rules-based order. But that is not the way India sees itself, as its refusal to follow America in condemning Russia over Ukraine makes clear. India is already a great power in its own right, and as it grows stronger still, its ambitions will grow too, and they will not be very different from China's. It too will seek a sphere of influence in its own region and try to keep other great powers out of it. So, far from aiming to support American primacy across the Indo-Pacific, India's priority will be to minimise other countries' power and influence in South Asia and the Indian Ocean, including America's. This means we should be approaching India not as an ally in the maintenance of the old order in Asia, but as a key part of the region's new, post-American order, and as a potential hegemon with ambitions for influence over us. We need to develop our own agenda to protect our interests from India, not falling for Washington's illusion of India as a loyal ally.

Likewise with Japan. For a long time now, and especially under Coalition governments, Canberra has talked up our strategic relationship with Japan, based on what it sees as a shared commitment to supporting America against China. But this greatly exaggerates how close the strategic partnership with Japan has become and fails to see how complex Japanese attitudes and approaches to China really are. Talk of a full-scale security alliance with Japan goes back to John Howard's last year in office in 2007, when he flew to Tokyo to sign a low-level agreement to facilitate routine defence contacts amid rumours that an ANZUS-like treaty was on the cards. Seven years ago, the relationship was being described as a "quasi-alliance." The Reciprocal Access Agreement signed with Tokyo in January 2022 has given rise to more of the same hyperbole. It is another purely administrative arrangement designed to help manage routine military-to-military connects. It embodies no strategic commitments at all. I'm sure Canberra is eager for a full alliance, but Japan remains evasive. Even to America, Japan has always been an elusive ally, happy to enjoy US support, but slow and reluctant to commit to support America in return. That is because Japan's strategic outlook is much more complex than either Canberra or Washington seems to appreciate. There are plenty of China hawks in Tokyo, but there are also many very influential figures who see workable relations with China as essential to Japan's future. Even the China hawks understand that China cannot simply be "contained" in the way many in Canberra and Washington imagine. Their objective is to construct the best possible long-term relationship with China in the light of the new realities of relative power between them. They are happy to use America's power to do that, but that is not the same as simply supporting Washington in whatever it does. There is a lot for Australia to learn from Japan's approach to China. But we will not do that as long as our US-centric outlook leads us to see Japan simply as a supporter of American primacy in Asia.

Then there is Southeast Asia. It should be obvious that the countries lying between Australia, China and India will be very important to us as we seek to manage our relations with Asia's two great powers. We have a lot in common with these neighbours. Like us, they are small or middle powers (except for Indonesia). Like us, they want to avoid falling under the shadow of either Beijing or Delhi. Unlike us, they understand that they are going to have to deal with this problem themselves, both individually and, to a degree, collectively. They are united in believing that it would be both futile and disastrous for America to try to contain China in a new Cold War.

Canberra has been in denial about this. It cites a series of ASEAN–Australia Summit meetings to claim that our Southeast Asian neighbours see the region's strategic challenges just the way we do. Our government seems to assume that beneath the euphemistic communiqué language about fostering peace and stability in the region, the Southeast Asians are committed to join us in doing whatever it takes to resist China's ambitions and preserve America primacy. But that assumption was sternly corrected by Prime Minister Lee Hsien Loong of Singapore in June 2021. With Morrison standing beside him, he delivered a stark and scarcely veiled rebuke to Australia's China policy. Asked, "What is your advice to Australia and the G7 on how to handle relationships with China?" he replied:

> You need to work with the country, it is going to be there, it is going to be a substantial presence and you can cooperate with it, you can engage it, you can negotiate with it. But it has to be a long and mutually constructive process. And you don't have to make it — You don't have to become like them, neither can you hope to make them become like you. And you have to be able to work on that basis.

It seems that Morrison, who was on his way to Cornwall, where he would seal the AUKUS deal, paid no attention to these words. That too has become the hallmark of Australia's regional diplomacy. We do no more than recite Washington's talking points to Southeast Asia's leaders, and they don't buy it. And then we do not listen to what they say to us in response. This is, in truth, simply following a pattern which has been set since the mid-1990s, when the energy and excitement which had powered our relationships in Southeast Asia began to drain away and we began to look again to America first. Now, as American power in Asia fades, those decades of needless neglect make it so much harder for us to build the relationships we will need to navigate the challenges ahead.

All that is especially true of Indonesia. Much has been written about our failure over many years to give Indonesia the weight it deserves. Here it is enough to say that the more difficult our strategic future in Asia looks, the more vital it becomes that we fix this and start to recognise just how important this enigmatic but powerful neighbour will be in a region no longer dominated by America. Our confidence in Washington has made us complacent about this as about so much else that is vital to our future.

And finally, there is the Southwest Pacific – "our Pacific family," as Scott Morrison insisted on calling it with more than a touch of his tactless paternalism. It has been entirely predictable that Canberra's engagement with our Pacific neighbours has revived as our fears of China's interest in them have grown. This follows a pattern stretching back to the mid-nineteenth century, when Australians first worried that potentially hostile major powers might build bases in the Southwest Pacific from which to attack us. Ever since then, Australia has tried to create a sphere of influence over these islands, claiming a right to exclude any major power from them except for our major allies. Our eagerness to enforce that has always been the primary driver of our involvement in the region, including our major colonial presence in Papua New Guinea. But our attention wandered from the early 1970s, when America's uncontested primacy in Asia allowed our fears to lapse. No country was going to defy America to intrude into "our backyard."

But now, of course, that is exactly what China is doing. In April 2018, it was reported that China wanted to build a military base in Vanuatu. Then in April 2022, the news broke that Solomon Islands had finalised a security agreement with China, which provided for a Chinese military and police presence and raised the possibility of a Chinese military base there. This detonated a grenade in the federal election campaign. Both sides agreed that it was a very dangerous development, reviving dim memories of the Pacific War and seeming to bring China's threat a lot closer to home. It also offered Labor a golden chance to deflect the government's attack on its national security credentials. Since the start of the year, Morrison and Dutton had made a big thing of claiming Labor was soft on China and arguing that only they could be trusted keep Australia safe. Now Labor argued that it was the Coalition that couldn't be trusted, and this hit home because Morrison had always made much of the priority he gave to keeping Australia's Pacific family in line. He responded to this setback by intemperately attacking the Solomon Islands government and declaring, "We won't be having Chinese military naval bases in our region on our doorstep." He even spoke of this being a "red line" for Australia – suggesting the use of force to prevent it. Labor promised it could fix the problem with more aid and better diplomacy.

In fact, neither the Coalition nor Labor has an answer to this problem. It marks a failure in Australia's long-term Pacific policy going back decades, to the times when the constellation of small nations across our north emerged from colonial rule as independent states. Canberra aimed to make Australia so appealing and indispensable to these new neighbours that they would never consider acting against our wishes or interests. But it has been clear for a long time – from the Fiji coups, for example, and PNG's war on Bougainville – that we haven't been succeeding. Over decades of neglect and paternalism, during which the development of these relationships has been subcontracted to the aid bureaucrats, our neighbours have learnt to see through our rhetoric and judge us by our actions – especially on issues where our policies so obviously hurt them, such as climate change. They have a keen sense of the shifting regional balance of power and an unsentimental approach to using it for their own ends. They will not be frightened into turning their backs on China by our dire warnings.

They are well used to the business of managing intrusive "great powers" who want to exercise undue influence – after all, they have been managing Australia for decades. And China has a lot to offer them, albeit not without some serious risks and potential downsides.

So what can we do? True to the logic of our alignment with Washington, Canberra's instinct is simply to tell our island neighbours to lock China out. That will not work. The new reality of power in Asia means that we no longer have the capacity to enforce a sphere of influence over our backyard. The old methods won't exclude a rival as powerful as China. So we are going to have to live with it. That is not perhaps as disastrous as many now assume. China's growing presence in our close neighbourhood – including a military presence – will increase its influence and will challenge us to lift our game to increase ours. But Chinese naval or air bases in places such as Solomon Islands are not as threatening to us militarily as many assume. We simply need to make sure that we have our own capacity to neutralise them early in a war, which should not be too hard. It calls for maritime forces that can deny an adversary access to such bases, and conventionally armed long-range strike forces – especially missiles – that can destroy them. These are capabilities that we need anyway to defend Australia itself.

COURAGE AND IMAGINATION

How do we get out of this mess?

The first step is to get real about the situation we face. We need to stop underestimating China's power and resolve, and overestimating America's, because a correct assessment of their relative positions is essential to understanding what is happening in Asia and how we can best respond. We have been getting these things wrong for too long. Like the rest of the West, we have eagerly believed the countless predictions that China's economic achievement was about to collapse or that its political system was about to implode. We have been equally eager to believe that under some future leadership China will abandon its ambitions. Of course these things could happen, but they haven't yet, and we would be unwise to bet that they will. We should by now have learnt that the only prudent basis for our policy is to accept that China will not collapse and its ambitions will not be abandoned. The China we see now is the China we must learn to live with.

Likewise, we have been too eager to accept, in the face of clear evidence, the comfortable consensus that America's position in Asia is invulnerable, that its armed forces are unbeatable and that its commitment to Asia is unshakable. We will never start to build ourselves a secure place in the new Asia until we banish these illusions. We need to get real, too, about how the rest of our region sees these issues. Far from being in the vanguard of a region united in its determination to resist China's ambition at all costs, we are an outlier in a region which is quietly getting on with the difficult business of adjusting to the new realities they seem to understand so much better than we do. We will not do better until we rid ourselves of the assumption – voiced recently, for example, by Dutton – that doubts about America's ability to prevail in Asia can only spring from deep-seated anti-Americanism. That lazy slur has been a barrier to serious thinking and debate for too long.

The second step is to build a more balanced and realistic view of China. Looking back, we may judge that the highly coloured and sometimes absurdly lurid description of China's threat to our sovereignty and way of life has served a useful purpose. It helped in overturning the complacent view – exemplified by Abbott's praise of Xi Jinping as a champion of democracy in 2014 – that China posed no challenge to the Asian order or Australia's interests. But predictably, things have now swung too far the other way. It is clear why this happened: we saw the same thing in the exaggerated threats of terrorism after 9/11. Once a rival or a threat is identified, it becomes all too easy to keep talking it up, and harder and harder to regain a sense of proportion. But as we found with the War on Terror, getting threats out of proportion leads to costly mistakes.

Of course, there is much we do not know and cannot know about how China's power and ambitions will develop. We do not know what kind of hegemon it will become, how far it will try to interfere in our internal affairs and how ruthless it will be in getting its way. It can seem safest in the face of these uncertainties to assume the worst and respond to China as if it were another Stalinist Russia or Nazi Germany. But worst cases do not always make for the best policy. On the contrary, they can lead to just the kind of costly mistakes we made in the War on Terror – but this time the costs could be quite literally catastrophic. A better approach is to recognise the range of possible outcomes and develop our policy accordingly. We should not rule out the worst cases, and we should prepare to respond to them if they occur. But if we base our policy entirely on the worst case – China as a ruthless and bitter enemy with which we cannot do business – then we have a good chance of that being what actually happens. So we should also recognise the clear possibility that China will turn out to be a regional hegemon we can learn to live with – if never to like much, let alone love – and build a policy towards that. In the simplest terms, this might mean that our defence policy should focus on the worst case and our diplomacy should focus on the better possibilities. But first we need to jettison the overhyped threats that dominate our view of China at present.

In doing that, it helps to keep China's power in proportion. Much of our debate sees China in two quite contradictory ways. On the one hand, it is a future global hegemon that threatens to take over the world and remake it according to the Chinese Communist Party's wishes. But at the same time, it is seen to be weaker and more fragile than it seems, unable to dominate even its own backyard and thus easy to deter or defeat. The reality we must adapt to is midway between these equally implausible extremes – a China strong enough to dominate our region, but not to rule the world.

The third step is to think seriously about war – major war between America and China – because the danger is real. It is clear from the way that political leaders and some senior officials have spoken about the prospect of war that they do not take it nearly as seriously as they should. One must suppose that they can scarcely imagine what war between nuclear-armed powers would be like – how it would be fought, how it would end, who would win and under what circumstances and for what ends it would be right to fight. Only when these things are understood can we make properly informed decisions about when and why we think such a war should be fought, and how hard we should work to avoid it. These are tough questions to answer, but the more clearly we understand what war would mean, the clearer the answers become. We are a long way from that kind of conversation in Australia today.

The fourth step is to talk to America about its future in Asia, and our role in sustaining it. That means doing more than just nodding along enthusiastically while our friends in Washington say their piece about how committed they are to staying the course. It means pressing them hard – harder than they seem to have pressed themselves – to explain what they are really trying to achieve and how they expect to achieve it. And if it turns out, for the reasons we have explored, that they have no good answers, then we need to urge them, for their good as well as ours, to think again. We need to make it crystal clear to them that they cannot expect Australia's support unless we are convinced that they have clear objectives and a realistic chance of achieving them at a cost and risk the American people are able and willing to bear over the long term.

This would be a most difficult conversation, because America is in a very difficult position. A lot has been said in recent years about how

US–China relations might fall into the "Thucydides Trap." This is the idea that war is inevitable when a rising power challenges an established power for preponderance in the international system – their rivalry traps them in a path to war they cannot escape. History gives a lot of support to the theory, because it has been so rare for an established great power to make way for a rising rival without a fight. The English scholar Martin Wight expressed this pithily in 1946 when he wrote, "Great power status is lost, as it is won, by violence. A great power does not die in its bed." But there are no iron laws of history, because what happens is always subject to some degree to human choice. Great powers have seldom in the past chosen to step back from a pinnacle of influence rather than go to war, but going to war is different now because of nuclear weapons. Ultimately, perhaps, that is why the Soviet Union did step back at the end of the Cold War. And ultimately the threat of nuclear war will convince the United States, if anything does, to step back from the contest with China over primacy in East Asia. That must be the hard advice that Australia offers Washington. If it cannot retain its position in Asia without running a serious risk of nuclear war, then it had better withdraw quickly and gracefully, because no one's interests are served by the alternative.

To be brutally realistic, that means, among other things, abandoning Taiwan to Beijing. That is hard to do, because it is easy to imagine how Taiwan would suffer under Beijing's rule. Perhaps it takes more effort to imagine how Taiwan would suffer in a nuclear war fought between America and China, especially one that America failed to win and which therefore left Taiwan not just devastated but abandoned to China anyway. But that is the effort we have to make, because that is the alternative we have to weigh if we are to make a responsible decision about our role and America's role in Taiwan's future. Some would say that the consequences of a war over Taiwan would be China's responsibility, because China would have started the war. There is a lot of truth in that, but it is not the whole truth. Any war results from choices made on both sides, and both sides bear responsibility for the choices when they decide that the costs of conflict are justified by the benefits. When those choices go wrong, there is plenty of blame to go around. No one today doubts that all sides share responsibility for the outbreak of war in 1914.

America faces these dilemmas over Taiwan because it has chosen for decades to make Taiwan's fate a test of its leadership in Asia. Responsibility for that lies with the generations of US policy-makers who perpetuated that choice. Those commitments made good sense when they were first made back in 1949, because the Cold War stakes for America were high and defending Taiwan from China was easy. But they stopped making sense a long time ago, as America's stakes in the situation fell and the costs of protecting Taiwan rose. The best way out of this predicament for America is to abandon ambiguity and acknowledge frankly that it cannot and will not defend Taiwan with armed force. And the best path for Australia is to urge America to do that and tell Americans plainly that we will not support them in a war over Taiwan.

It is a long time since we spoke to our allies in Washington like this. But then it is a long time since the stakes were so high, since they made the kinds of demands of us they are making now, and since it was so unclear that they can deliver what they promise. However, this does not mean that we should, in effect, tell America to leave Asia. It is plainly in our interests for America to preserve the strongest possible strategic role in our region that is consistent with a stable, non-adversarial relationship with China. As we have seen, it will now be hard to convince Beijing to scale back its ambitions for regional hegemony by accepting a significant US strategic role in East Asia and the Western Pacific. Hard, but perhaps not impossible, so it is clearly worth trying. We should urge America to do that by exploring, with realistic expectations and an open mind, what kind of understandings might be reached with Beijing.

Nor should we take the initiative to abandon our alliance with America. The argument to be made for that radical step is that entanglements like Pine Gap would inevitably drag us into an American war with China whether we decided to take part or not. I think that risk is exaggerated.

If we are smart and tough, we can manage our alliance commitments to preserve our freedom of choice in a crisis. As long as we can do that, it will not make sense to abandon the alliance, because we can always benefit from a close relationship with a country which will remain among the three richest and most powerful in the world. But what we must not do, as I have argued throughout this essay, is to assume that America will not abandon us.

The fifth step in getting real is to recast our diplomacy in Asia. We should talk to India not just as a Quad partner and a counterbalance to China but as a great power with its own great-power objectives. We should try to understand the complexities of Japan's attitudes to China and options for dealing with it. We should stop telling our Southeast Asian neighbours that US primacy is the only path to regional order and start listening to them about how they see China's and India's rises and how they are dealing with them. We should stop telling our South Pacific neighbours to keep their distance from China and start working hard to become a more rewarding partner ourselves. And we should take the trouble to chat to New Zealand's leaders as well, because they seem to have done a much better job of managing China than we have. They have stood up to China where it matters without destroying their relationship, by avoiding point-scoring provocations and keeping a prudent distance from Washington's containment policies. They might have something to teach us.

And sixth, obviously, we have to start talking to China. This will not be easy, but there is no alternative. It will not work to insist — as both sides of politics do — that Beijing must take the steps required to get us back into the room together, because fundamentally they are more important to us than we are to them. So we should respond to such openings as Beijing offers — for example, the clear efforts by China's current ambassador to restore some dialogue. It is a sign of weakness to refuse to talk.

But before we start talking seriously to China, or indeed to anyone else, we need to a conversation among ourselves — a national conversation — about how Australia should respond to the biggest shift in our international environment since Europeans settled on this continent. That is the conversation that our political leaders have been ducking for years, first by denying that we had any choices to make, and then by asserting that the only choice we could possibly make is to back America in whatever it decides to do. Now it's time to start talking about the real choices we have to make.

That is a task for political leaders, and the way for them to begin is to set out in plain terms the essentials of our situation. They can be easily summarised. The rise of China, of India and in time of Indonesia are among the biggest geopolitical shifts in history, and they will not be reversed. As a result, the strategic order in Asia which frames Australia's place in the world has already changed and the old order will not return. We know for sure that India and China will play a greater role in this new order than any other countries, and we have to learn to live with them and work with them. This will be very different from the orders we have known and it will be hard to adjust. But there is no sense in exaggerating the threats we face. We should continue to hope that America will plays a substantial role in Asia's new order, but we should not simply rely on America to keep Asia safe for us in future. We will have to build our own relationships with the new great powers of Asia and find new ways to work with our many old friends among Asia's smaller and middle powers to promote the interests we share. Above all, we must do whatever we can to ensure that the transition to a new order happens peacefully, because we must be under no illusion that war would solve anything.

It should not be too hard to draft a speech along these lines, if we could only find a political leader willing to deliver it.

This task is Labor's duty, and its opportunity, as it takes power. It is a task for which Labor should be well fitted by its history. Curtin's statesmanship in war, Evatt's acerbic creativity in shaping the post-war order, Calwell's principled and perceptive opposition to Vietnam, Whitlam's far-sighted and courageous opening to China, Hawke and Keating's inspired realisation of Australia's Asian future, Gareth Evans' mastery of principled, practical diplomacy. There is a lot to build on here.

But it is a long time now since Labor had a foreign policy it could call its own. In office between 2007 and 2013, it followed the policies set by Howard, making no effort to rethink or correct the grave errors that led, for example, to the debacle in Afghanistan. In Opposition it sat on the sidelines for the past five years as Australia's relations with China, and any coherent vision of our future in Asia, collapsed. It never criticised the substance of the Morrison government's policies in China, but merely quibbled about the tone. It rushed to endorse AUKUS within a few hours of its announcement. It never questioned, indeed repeatedly endorsed, the assumption that America will solve our China problem for us.

How deep this assumption goes was revealed in the midst of the election campaign when Penny Wong was interviewed by Leigh Sales on 7.30 about China and Solomon Islands. Wong channelled a former US Secretary of State, the late Madelaine Albright, when she said to Sales, "The United States is the indispensable nation when it comes to security in our region and obviously in the world." It was just a line in a TV interview, but it was a revealing remark nonetheless. In 1998, at the height of America's post–Cold War strength and optimism, Albright famously used that phrase to claim for America the leadership of the world: "We are America; we are the indispensable nation. We stand tall and we see further than other countries into the future." A lot of people thought like that in 1998, but much has changed since then. To speak of America today in these terms, as "indispensable," suggests an inability to see how much has changed – how far we are now from that 1998 vision of America as the new Rome standing unchallenged and unchallengeable at the apex of the global order. It suggests an inability to imagine how we in Australia can make our way in Asia and the world without relying on America to make our way for us. But that is exactly what we have to do, as Labor should realise.

Its refusal to do so is partly political calculation. Mark Latham was the last Labor leader to allow daylight to appear between Labor's foreign and defence policies and the Coalition's, but more to indulge his blokey iconoclasm than to promote a coherent policy alternative. His failure as

Labor leader only reinforced what was already a strong conviction across the party's factions that it was electoral suicide for Labor to do anything but mirror Coalition positions, especially in the era of the War on Terror. This caution has been nourished by tribal memories of the 1960s, when Labor was repeatedly kept from office by its principled opposition to Coalition foreign and defence policies. The result is an unshakable, or at least untested, conviction that Labor, in or out of power, cannot win or hold government without copying the Coalition's foreign policy. That is why there is no area of policy in which Labor's small-target political strategy has been applied more ruthlessly than in foreign and defence policy. At a time of extraordinary dangers and challenges, Labor has deserted the policy debate and called it bipartisanship – except when it suits them to play politics themselves, as they did over Solomon Islands.

But there is more to this than political timidity. For many in Labor, it is a matter of conviction. Most of those who speak most often on foreign policy eagerly assert their passionate belief in US leadership and their support for America against China. Some have made a point of criticising Coalition governments for not going far enough in supporting America against China. In 2016, for example, Labor's Richard Marles urged the government to order the ADF to undertake more assertive freedom-of-navigation operations against China in the South China Sea. This is perhaps not surprising. Labor's leading figures today came of age politically well after the end of the Hawke/Keating era, and they misread the political and policy lessons to be learnt from it. Hawke and Keating built Labor's credentials as a capable custodian of defence and foreign policy by embracing the US alliance, but they never did so as uncritically as their successors do now. And back then America's uncontested primacy in Asia really did mean the alliance could guarantee our security.

Last year Anthony Albanese responded to Paul Keating's trenchant criticisms of Labor's positions on China and America by saying that a lot had changed since Keating was in power. And yet it is Albanese and his colleagues who, at least until now, have clung to a vision of the world and Australia's place in it that dates back to the 1980s and 1990s.

Will they do better in government? The good news is that Labor will be less tempted than the Morrison government was to exacerbate tensions with Beijing to score political points at home. We may therefore hope for a little easing of hostility, which Beijing may well be willing to reciprocate, leading to the restoration of some diplomatic engagement. But nothing fundamental will have changed. Albanese's language as he flew off to the Quad summit in Tokyo reflected his instinct to stick closely to the lines laid down by his predecessor. If so, he will do nothing to address the underlying problems in our relations with China and in our broader foreign, strategic and defence policies. That will require the kind of steps sketched in the last few pages, which will demand real courage and effort and leadership – what used to be called "statesmanship." Do Albanese and his team have it in them? We shall see. For all the urgency of the other issues that crowd in upon them as they take office, this may well prove to be the one that most defines the Albanese government and frames its legacy.

But this is not just a challenge for Labor. The Coalition, as it rebuilds and redefines itself in Opposition, will need to think carefully about how far to stick with the policies on China and America that it fell into during its last few years in office. It will be interesting to see how far it tries to block Labor moves to a more sophisticated and far-sighted policy by maintaining the jingoistic posturing we saw from Morrison and Dutton. The Liberals might reflect not just on what would best serve Australia's interests, but what would serve their party's, because it would be surprising if Dutton's eager war-talk did not help to swing votes to the Greens and Teals on 21 May 2022.

And then there are the Greens and Teals themselves. Whether their remarkable success in the year's election really heralds a seismic shift in our national politics depends partly on whether they contribute to, and help shape, national debates on questions beyond the specific issues they campaigned on. None of them have yet had much to say about the great issues of foreign and strategic policy that we face. That should change if they are to do their duty and fulfil their potential.

Back in 2010 I concluded my first Quarterly Essay, *Power Shift*, with these words: "We need to accept that if China keeps growing, and it probably will, Asia will change. For Australia, foreign and defence policy are getting serious again." I'll say it again.

SOURCES

2   Recent figures: Department of Foreign Affairs and Trade, *An Update to An India Economic Strategy to 2035: Navigating from potential to delivery*, Commonwealth of Australia, Canberra, p. 12.

6   "comprehensive strategic partnership": Julia Gillard, Statement, 26 June 2013.

7   major speech in Singapore: Malcolm Turnbull, Keynote address at the 16th IISS Asia Security Summit, Shangri-La Dialogue, 3 June 2017.

8   "Fear and greed": John Garnaut, "'Fear and greed' drive Australia's China policy, Tony Abbott tells Angela Merkel", *The Sydney Morning Herald*, 16 April 2015.

8   "Australia doesn't have to choose": Phillip Coorey, "Scott Morrison: 'We won't choose' between US, China", *Australian Financial Review*, 16 November 2018.

9   "reset" speech: Malcolm Turnbull, Speech at the University of New South Wales, Sydney, 7 August 2018.

9   "They do see us": Peter Dutton, National Press Club Address, Canberra, ACT, 26 November 2021.

9   he warned again: Bryant Hevesi, "'Prepare for war': Peter Dutton issues ominous warning – as he says China is 'on a very deliberate course at the moment'", Sky News online, 25 April 2022.

10   "most significant step": Tom Mcillroy, "AUKUS is the most significant step of our time, says Dutton", *Australian Financial Review*, 26 October 2021.

10   "single greatest initiative": Scott Morrison, press conference, Canberra, ACT, 16 September 2021.

10   "The secretary's position": Matthew Knott, "Independence actually: Marise Payne's unmistakable message to the US", *The Sydney Morning Herald*, 29 July 2020.

11   "Foreign policy consists": Walter Lippman, *American Foreign Policy: Shield of the Republic*, Little, Brown & Co, 1943, p. 9.

13   Australia's 1994 Defence White Paper: Commonwealth of Australia, *Defending Australia 1994*, Canberra, 1994, pp. 8–9.

13   warning explicitly: Aaron Friedberg, "Will Europe's past be Asia's future?", *Global Politics and Strategy*, vol. 42, no. 3, 2000, pp. 147–60.

15   They say: Kurt M. Campbell and Ely Ratner, "The China reckoning: How Beijing defied American expectations", *Foreign Affairs*, 13 February 2018.

17   Trump administration's National Security Strategy: *National Security Strategy of the United States of America*, December 2017.

17   America's highest: The Joint Chiefs of Staff, Description of the Military Strategy 2018, Strategy Development Division Deputy Directorate for Joint Strategic Planning Directorate for Strategy, Plans, and Policy.

17 *Strategic Framework*: US Strategic Framework for the Indo-Pacific, https://trumpwhitehouse.archives.gov/wp-content/uploads/2021/01/IPS-Final-Declass.pdf, accessed 18 May 2022. See also, as examples of the paperwork coming out of Washington under the Trump administration, https://trumpwhitehouse.archives.gov/wp-content/uploads/2020/05/U.S.-Strategic-Approach-to-The-Peoples-Republic-of-China-Report-5.24v1.pdf and https://www.state.gov/wp-content/uploads/2019/11/Free-and-Open-Indo-Pacific-4Nov2019.pdf.

18 step back: Marise Payne and Secretary of State Mike Pompeo, press conference, Sydney, 29 July 2020.

18 "extreme competition": "Biden: China should expect 'extreme competition' from US", *The Sydney Morning Herald*, 8 February 2021.

19 "to win the twenty-first century": Liam O'Dell, "Biden singles out China as global competition to 'win 21st century'", *The Independent*, www.independent.co.uk/tv/news/biden-singles-out-china-as-global-competition-to-win-21st-century--v637e20e3, accessed 18 May 2022.

19 "Decline": Charles Krauthammer, "Decline is a choice", *Washington Examiner*, 19 October 2009.

20 "the rules, values, and relationships": Antony J. Blinken, "A Foreign Policy for the American People", speech, 3 March 2021.

20 "As President": Barack Obama, "Remarks in Address to the Nation on the Way Forward in Afghanistan and Pakistan", 1 December 2009.

23 Beijing might lock US firms out: Elbridge A. Colby, *The Strategy of Denial: American defense in an age of great power conflict*, Yale, 2012, pp. 10 ff.

26 "It was essential": George F. Kennan, *American Diplomacy 1900-1950*, Chicago, 1951, p. 5.

26 If it could: Adan Tooze, *The Deluge: The Great War and the Remaking of Global Order*, Penguin Books, 2014, p. 161.

27 "entire security as a nation": "X" [George F. Kennan], "The sources of Soviet conduct", *Foreign Affairs*, July 1947.

29 "start by moving away": Kurt M. Campbell and Rush Doshi, "How America Can Shore Up Asian Order", *Foreign Affairs*, 12 January 2021.

29 "the one central theme": Michael J. Green, *By More Than Providence: Grand strategy and American power in the Asia Pacific since 1783*, Columbia, NY, 2019, p. 5.

29–30 the most sophisticated contemporary account: Colby, *The Strategy of Denial*, Chapter 1.

31 China wants to: Kevin Rudd, *The Avoidable War: The dangers of a catastrophic conflict Between the US and Xi Jinping's China*, Hachette, Sydney, 2022, Chapter 17.

34 "must work out": Lee Hsien Loong, "The endangered Asian century", *Foreign Affairs*, 4 June 2020.

38	"common-sense guardrails": Joe Biden's Virtual Meeting with President Xi Jinping of the People's Republic of China, 16 November 2021.
40	"Victory would be bought": Winston Churchill, *The Great War*, vol. 1, London, 1934, p. 495.
41	best recent study of US military strategy against China: Colby, *The Strategy of Denial*, Chapter 5.
50	"a tragic mistake": Thomas L. Friedman, "This is Putin's war", *The New York Times*, 21 February 2022.
51	"We want to see": Secretary of State Antony J. Blinken and Secretary of Defense Lloyd J. Austin III, Remarks to traveling press, 25 April 2022.
59	"this was", "were the ultimate defenders" and "categorical spelling out": Kerry Brown, "War represents a failure of diplomacy. It pays to read past page one", *The Interpreter*, The Lowy Institute, 31 March 2022.
62	Recent estimates: DFAT, *An Update to An India Economic Strategy to 2035*, p. 12.
65	"a question for the Chinese": Samantha Maiden, "Peter Dutton's blunt warning over prospect of war with China", News.com.au, 17 September 2021.
65	"inconceivable": Reuters, "'Inconceivable' Australia would not join US to defend Taiwan", *Australian Financial Review*, 13 November 2021.
66	our eagerness to fight in 1914: Douglas Newton, *Hell Bent: Australia's leap into the Great War*, Melbourne, 2014.
69	heading for 2.5 per cent: Tom McIlroy, "Defence spending to reach $50 billion a year says Dutton", *Australian Financial Review*, 26 October 2021.
72	for the price: Hugh White, "SSN versus SSK", *The Interpreter*, Lowy Institute, 29 September 2021.
75	"quasi-alliance": John Garnaut, "Australia–Japan military ties are a 'quasi-alliance', say officials", *The Sydney Morning Herald*, 26 October 2014.
76	"You need to": Prime Minister Scott Morrison and Prime Minister Lee Hsieng Loong, press conference, 11 June 2026.
77	Much has been written: For example, *Australian Foreign Affairs*, Issue 3, July 2018.
77	Australia has tried to create a sphere of influence: Our Sphere of Influence, *Australian Foreign Affairs*, Issue 6, July 2019.
79	capabilities that we need anyway: Hugh White, *How to Defend Australia*, Latrobe University Press, 2019, Chapter 10.
83	"Great power status": Martin Wight, *Power Politics*, Royal Institute of International Affairs, 1946, p. 21.
87	"The United States is the indispensable nation": Penny Wong, 7.30, ABC TV, 20 April 2022.
87	"we are America": Secretary of State Madeleine Albright, Interview on *The Today Show*, NBC TV, 19 February 1998.

Rick Morton

Reading Sarah Krasnostein's beautiful, sick-making Quarterly Essay, *Not Waving, Drowning*, in a local park beneath dappled autumn light, I was reminded how much of my relatively good mental health now is simply the product of time, money and language.

It wasn't always this way.

When Orygen's director of clinical services, Dr Andrew Chanen, tells Krasnostein that "a lot of the problems associated with BPD [borderline personality disorder] are not part of the diagnostic criteria," it made me sit upright, leaning into the revelation of those words.

The constellation of confusing presentations to emergency departments, the "difficult" behaviour of people seeking help – none of this is necessarily inherent in BPD, as Chanen says, but in "things that we create."

"They're diagnostic of the mental health system," he says.

And, as the essay addresses, these harms are inflicted well beyond the mental health system silo. They are all around us.

During the promotional run for *My Year of Living Vulnerably* – a book I wrote to make sense of my recent diagnosis with complex post-traumatic stress disorder (cPTSD), a condition with very close links to the BPD of Krasnostein's impressive case study Eliza – I spoke offhand about the seven or so psychologists and psychiatrists I had seen over the course of a decade in a bid to get better. Because I had initially been diagnosed with depression and an anxiety disorder all the way back at university, this was the label that stuck. And that, apparently, would have been the end of the matter if, at age thirty and armed with hard-won knowledge, I had not finally demanded a reappraisal.

After one radio interview, I received an email.

"I was that uni psychologist that stuck those very sticky and unhelpful labels on you. At the time, as a CBT [cognitive behaviour therapy] therapist, that's all

I could really see to fit with our brief discussions. How much more I know today," the psychologist wrote.

"Anyway, I just felt compelled to say I'm sorry I didn't know or have the time to help you understand that little seven-year-old Rick, that vulnerable little boy, was still showing up, and we needed to work together to help him feel safe and connected."

To be clear, I have never once blamed this person. They, too, were the product of an inelegant system designed to spit out inelegant solutions. And they are, through this kind of eternal curiosity, a force for good. But it is true, too, that those original sticky labels produced something of a tunnel for my own treatment. I have been on medication – SSRIs, once daily – for seven years, although it is now clear they were not needed. These pills produce terrifying withdrawals. The CBT so favoured by Medicare is not particularly well suited to treating trauma-related conditions: there are better options. In my lost decade, I didn't even know to ask for them. Like Eliza, there was no language available to me for what had happened and nobody, in all my frenzied interactions with the system, who could speak it.

What is maddening about all of this, as Krasnostein correctly observes, is that we have arranged our collective social mind to hide away the uncomfortable truths about mental illness. It feels too big, I suppose, to stare down the role of poverty; family dysfunction; the harsh illogic of the justice system; chronic pain and physical ailments; the stress of being any kind of "other"; physical or emotional traumas; and government systems meant – at least in our conception of them – to provide support but which come booby-trapped by negligence or, worse, malicious intent (Robodebt, anyone?), such that they can grind the very objects of their attention into paste.

Yes, it all sounds very hard.

So we open a new Headspace, launch the 874th awareness campaign and double the number of Medicare-rebated psychological sessions in a given year to twenty. More of the same, with the same results. Of course, some of the approaches that will make a difference are not very "hard" at all. It just takes money. Not only in mental health but to pay people enough through the safety net that they are not destitute. That is, payments above the Henderson poverty line. Housing that is affordable and accessible; services in justice that do not, as Krasnostein writes, "mistake the last note for the whole song." So much of our public expenditure is, in the old parlance of health bureaucracy, sending ambulances to wait at the bottom of the cliff. It has become fashionable to frame these moral truths in the language of ideology. Unemployment benefits, according to some, are not meant to be "easy" to live on because then people might actually manage to live on them. But if you're not inclined to believe the bleeding hearts, ask the hard-headed economists and researchers at the Productivity Commission whom Krasnostein quotes at length. Loath to use the terms of neoliberalism though I am, this argument from conservatives and reactionaries is lost even on the doctrines of their sacred economic temples.

What we continue to ignore is making us sicker.

I think of all this when I am reading Krasnostein's QE in the park on an afternoon when, despite recently living through one of the most multidimensionally stressful periods of my adult life, the earth does not threaten to swallow me whole. The ground does not tremble, precisely because I am lucky. To have work that I am able to do, that I enjoy doing and that pays me well. Work that allows me to look after my family and preserve their dignity in the face of otherwise diabolical circumstances. My being here, reading this clarifying essay, is pot luck. Still, despite working myself raw in fear of losing the only thing that afforded me a skerrick of agency in my own life – my job – there were so many months where it almost all came undone. Months where I spent every last cent I earned on out-of-pockets, running the roulette of bulk-billed GPs wherever in Australia I could walk in when needed. One of them kicked me out of his office when I asked for a new mental healthcare plan, because that would have taken fifteen minutes and he hadn't had lunch.

On paper I was income middle class, albeit with none of the structural advantages of those born into this category, and still I was drowning. What hope the millions of Australians with fewer resources? With deeper and more complex layers of hurt?

Instead of offering them a hand in the churning water, we're commenting on their stroke. Lazy, defective, morally culpable perhaps. This kind of thinking is baked into public life.

A little love, in the sense that love is a way of saying I *see* you, would remove at least some of this degrading nonsense. But as anyone who has ever loved anyone in any way knows, it can be difficult to inhabit the lonely chambers of that place.

"Ignore words and look at outcomes," NSW Hunter Region GP Adrian Plaskett tells Sarah Krasnostein. "For the health system, have a think about areas that work really well. Emergency – you have a car accident, you have a heart attack – we have extraordinarily good outcomes in Australia. Intensive care – does a wonderful job.

"Any sort of emergency surgery – public health is great. Cancer is pretty good – my sister had breast cancer last year and it all went pretty smoothly. And then ask yourself: what are the parts of the hospital that the middle class uses? There it is. What are the parts of the hospital that poorer people use? There it is."

This is a shameful state of affairs when we know, in our sinew, that people help create governments, and governments can help engineer a little luck. When we and they manage to do this, however, we call it something else.

We call it help. We call it love.

Rick Morton

Jennifer Doggett

For those (like me) who work within the health sector, mental health is a puzzle.

It's an area where there is a surprising level of agreement among stakeholders. Politicians (from both sides of politics), clinicians and consumers all seem united in their concern about the rates of both mental illness and sub-clinical mood disorders in Australian society. It's also an issue which has been a high personal priority for individual health ministers (including the recent federal Minister for Health, Greg Hunt), who have allocated significant policy, political and financial resources to improve our mental health outcomes.

In any other area of health, these factors would have resulted in substantial progress. But in mental health, they appear to have delivered only marginal gains.

Also puzzling is that, unlike the other public health challenges we face (such as obesity, smoking and Covid-19), the causes of our seemingly intractable mental health problems are murky.

From the outside, there is no clear reason why Australians are experiencing so much mental distress. Australia outperforms the OECD average in income, jobs, education, health, environmental quality, social connections, civic engagement and life satisfaction. Even accounting for the impact of the Covid-19 pandemic, Australians have never lived longer, with greater health and more material wealth than they do today.

Yet rates of depression and anxiety are at record levels, seemingly even higher than those of many other countries with materially worse living standards and conditions – Indonesia, Nigeria and Mexico, for example (although, due to data quality issues, it can be difficult to make accurate comparisons across countries).

Suicide is the leading cause of death among Australians aged fifteen to twenty-four, with rates among young Aboriginal and Torres Strait Islander people double that of non-Indigenous young people. Domestic violence (which often results from and in turn causes or exacerbates mental health problems) is a national emergency:

on average, one woman a week is murdered by her current or former partner.

Everyone agrees that these are serious and urgent problems. But disagreements arise as to their cause and therefore possible solutions. People on the left cite social determinants such as rising inequality, poverty and racism as the main drivers of mental health problems. Those on the other end of the political spectrum point to the shift in social institutions such as marriage and family or our changing views about gender. Others suggest environmental issues and the existential threat posed by climate change. It seems that mental illness is a mirror which reflects back to the viewer their existing concerns, anxieties and ideologies. In this way it reinforces the ideologies and worldviews which divide us, making it difficult to work together to develop a common response.

Sarah Krasnostein's thoughtful and wide-ranging essay sheds some useful light on this problem and suggests where our previous approaches to mental health may have gone wrong. By stepping outside the conventional, individualistic and health-centred approach to mental illness, she draws connections between our traumatic past as a nation and our current struggles with mental illness today. She highlights the importance, at both an individual and a social level, of naming and responding to trauma, and describes how this can contribute to our understanding of mental illness.

Obviously, mental health policies, programs and services can be important in addressing mental health needs, and Krasnostein is certainly not suggesting otherwise. But her essay also makes clear how anaemic these responses are when they are seen outside of a broader context: the traumas of our past, the fault-lines of race, class, gender and sexuality, and our collective anxieties about existential threats of climate change, the Covid-19 pandemic and global conflicts.

As we grapple with the findings of the Royal Commission into Victoria's Mental Health System, Krasnostein demonstrates why this issue is too important to be left to the policy-makers, clinicians, bureaucrats and politicians.

It illustrates how desperately we need the knowledge and wisdom of those not generally included in the mental health debate: the historians, the storytellers, the educators, the grandmothers and elders. It reminds us how much we can learn from the resilience of Indigenous, migrant and refugee communities about the strength of shared stories and the healing power of relationships.

Most significantly of all, Krasnostein highlights the importance of listening to the voices and experiences of people living with trauma and mental illness – people like Eliza, Daylia, Rebecca and Codey, whose stories Krasnostein respectfully and sensitively shares. Along with her deep insights and thoughtful analysis, their stories provide a powerful and valuable reminder of the human and social cost of our failure to address the impact of mental illness on the Australian community.

Jennifer Doggett

Russell Marks

Sarah Krasnostein's essay makes many important observations about Australia's mental health system and the people caught up within it. Stigma endures despite decades of awareness campaigns, partly because of the competing need – often expressed through News Corp's papers and commercial TV current affairs – to moralise, to punish and to stoke fear. Like every other funded service, mental health is subject to the dictates of administrative gatekeepers who are the foot soldiers of the neoliberal revolution. Often this produces contradictions. Governments point to the extra millions and billions they're investing in mental health, but people trying to access those resources need to jump through ever more hoops. Neoliberal ideology doesn't allow the provision of a universal public service for a universal public benefit, so people who have the least means to stay afloat end up drowning in tides of bureaucratic "criteria": mental healthcare plans; Centrelink applications and assessments; bureaucratically imposed geographic boundaries; non-government organisations which will do this but not that; never-ending waiting lists. Stable housing is now fairly universally recognised as the main precursor to stable mental health. Fifty years into the neoliberal revolution, our system of housing, as Krasnostein repeatedly observes, is now entirely broken.

For all practical purposes, there are two mental health systems in Australia. There's a system for people who can pay private psychiatrists and psychologists, and then there's the public system. Many people who find themselves engaging – as patients or as their families or friends – with the public system in most parts of the country are bewildered at the lengths to which it goes to apparently keep people sick.

Throughout 2020 I worked for a publicly funded legal service in a capital city (not Melbourne), representing people with diagnosed mental illnesses and intellectual disabilities. Among the extraordinary powers doctors have under state and territory legislation is the ability to "section" patients: to subject them to involuntary psychiatric treatment and to detain them in a hospital in order to effect it. (The colloquial term "section" is shorthand for the particular legislative clauses – they're different in each state's *Mental Health Act* – which authorise these actions.) To ensure doctors aren't using those powers unnecessarily, all involuntary treatment orders are automatically subject to periodic review by mental health tribunals. What I learnt in my year in those tribunals was that any transparency and accountability they appeared to provide was mostly a façade. In practice, nobody wanted to second-guess the original doctor's decision to make the order. Patients had a right to a second medical opinion, but invariably that opinion would be provided by the first doctor's colleague, in the same hospital.

Patients under involuntary treatment orders are chronically gaslit. I saw patients who were routinely punished for merely asking questions of their psychiatrists, whose progress reports to tribunals would claim that patients "did not accept" their diagnoses and therefore "lacked insight" into their conditions. "Insight," it turns out, is fundamentally important in public psychiatry. As far as I could tell, a patient with "insight" is one who dutifully and unquestioningly accepts their diagnosis (even if it's a vague and imprecise one like "schizoaffective disorder"), their treatment (even if it's a heavy dose of psychotropic medication which causes them to gain weight rapidly, lose the ability to orgasm and sleep all the time) and their environment (even if it's a closed hospital ward). These dutiful patients were obviously easier to deal with, so they got an easier run: nice things would be written about them in progress reports, and tribunal members would smile and say encouraging things. Patients who asked questions, or who became frustrated, or who disputed their diagnosis would invariably be accused of "lacking insight," which meant they couldn't possibly be ready to progress to a less restrictive form of treatment.

Psychiatry is necessarily an inexact science. It's common for psychiatrists to disagree about diagnoses and treatment, because the same symptoms are often consistent with a range of conditions. But consult two psychiatrists who are colleagues in the same public hospital system, and the second will invariably concur with the first.

Very occasionally I'd have a client who was able to secure – by paying for it – a second opinion from a private psychiatrist who was entirely independent of the public hospital treating team. This was rare: the professional world of psychiatry is a small one. But this was practically the only way of problematising the narratives created by the public hospital treating teams. If the private psychiatrist recommended less restrictive treatment, the tribunal was generally obliged to endorse it. So middle-class clients were sometimes able to find a crack in the walls erected by the public treating teams. But schizophrenia isn't generally a middle-class disorder. Strongly correlated with severe childhood trauma, it most often afflicts people in poverty, or causes middle-class sufferers to sink into poverty. Most of my clients had no access to a private psychiatrist. They simply had to cope with the demands of their hospital treating teams.

The general rule – compliance good, questions bad – seemed to me to be entirely the wrong way round. Surely it's outside the normal range of human experience to be confronted with a complete lack of freedom and respond with total submission? Yet over and over again, that's what public psychiatrists and mental health tribunals appeared to demand. Over time, some of my clients learnt what was expected of them, and played along. When they spoke to me, they would express the kinds of doubt and rage I'd normally expect from anyone forced to take debilitating meds and prevented from going outside. To their doctors and nurses and social workers, they'd say "yes ma'am, no sir, three bags full." Invariably, these patients would slowly progress to less restrictive treatment.

In her essay, Krasnostein points to a possible motive other than clinical need which might account for this common experience among public mental health patients: power and control. My socio-economic status is such that I occasionally mix socially with doctors. In my experience, doctors are rarely democratically inclined. I've often wondered whether this is a necessary corollary of being required to make very quick life-and-death decisions, for which self-doubt must be entirely unhelpful. When they debrief after shifts, it's often to express a kind of outrage that a mere patient or their family dared question their expert assessment. One doctor told me once of his discomfort when he discovered that a more senior colleague had made a potentially life-threatening error. During the exchange which ensued, the doctor told me he'd "never" report a colleague, and would "always" endorse that colleague's medical opinion to the patient, even if he suspected or knew it was wrong. Medical culture, I suspect, has a lot to answer for.

Occasionally I have met doctors who seem genuinely committed to involving their patients – and their very human fears, uncertainties, doubts, questions and, yes, even rages – in decisions which will affect them. Often in public psychiatry this simply isn't possible, because many patients are very unwell. But even when confronted with a schizophrenic patient in the florid throes of a psychotic episode, surely the public mental health system has more to offer than bed restraints and forced injections in an austere ward?

One of my clients, who had migrated from Tanzania, was on very high doses of antipsychotic medication to treat her "treatment-resistant" schizophrenia. (I was never able to resolve this contradiction: why continue to inject medication with strong side effects into patients whose conditions aren't responding to it?) She constantly reported feeling lonely, depressed and hopeless, which she said was due to the fact that she couldn't see a way out of her very restrictive existence. She wanted to return to Tanzania, but that option was never seriously considered by her treating team. (In his remarkable book *Crazy Like Us: The Globalization of the American Psyche*, Ethan Watters observes that non-Western cultures often respond rather less restrictively to what the DSM describes as "schizophrenia.") She died suddenly while waiting for her umpteenth six-monthly tribunal review. I strongly suspected suicide, but I wasn't allowed to know her cause of death.

Another client, also diagnosed with treatment-resistant schizophrenia, often told me of feeling hopeless and lonely, and said that he was consumed by memories of the horrific abuse he endured as a child. I obviously couldn't know whether those memories were true or symptomatic of his schizophrenia, but I was struck by his treating team's unwillingness even to attempt to obtain any collateral information. While he broadly understood the need for his antipsychotic medication, he also consistently requested grief and trauma counselling, or at least "someone to talk to." His doctor told me that there's no evidence that talking therapy has any clinical benefit for schizophrenia. Indeed, none of my clients in the public mental health system were ever able to access regular counselling or psychological therapy: it's been well documented that public health psychiatry has moved a long way from its psychoanalytic origins, and now seems to consist of a trial-and-error approach to the various pharmacological alternatives currently available. My client's entire experience of the public mental health system was as an involuntary patient who was punished with hospital admissions whenever he didn't show up to his fortnightly depo injection, which (for him) never did much other than make him sleep all day and night. His was an almost unimaginably bleak existence.

Another client, also diagnosed with schizophrenia, had been considered "treatment-resistant" until the advent of the NDIS, when he began to gradually take control of his therapy and his life with the help of a trusted support coordinator. He'd occasionally say strange things, but the proof was in the pudding: after being consistently in and out of jail since he was a teenager, he hadn't been so much as arrested since his NDIS package commenced. I've never met a worthier poster child for the NDIS. His treating team, however, found both him and his support coordinator difficult to deal with. So it applied to the civil and administrative tribunal to have the Public Guardian take over his NDIS decision-making. At law, guardianship orders can only be made when there is positive evidence that a person lacks the capacity to make decisions. Yet in my experience, treating teams would make applications when their patients were making NDIS decisions the teams simply didn't agree with. Eventually we persuaded the tribunal to dismiss the applications, though not without a fight and fifteen pages of written submissions.

Some treating teams would refuse to abide by tribunals' dismissals of their guardianship applications. Upon having their applications dismissed, they would simply make new ones. My client in the paragraph above had endured four such applications by the time I met him. Another client, who had a severe intellectual disability, had been subject to rolling guardianship applications by his doctors. After removing him from his mother's care as a child, the Department of Child Safety had placed him in a now-notorious children's home, in which he endured seven years of physical and sexual abuse. When he turned eighteen, the Public Guardian simply warehoused him in a locked facility operated by the Department of Disability Services for almost a decade, before his mother first won guardianship back and then got him out of the secure facility, after which his behaviour – hitherto deemed intractably bad by his treating team – began to improve. But his doctors didn't like his mother. So they tried over and over again – five times, by our first meeting – to have his guardianship returned to the Public Guardian. Within a month of the tribunal's most recent decision, which appointed his mother as guardian for the maximum period (five years), his doctors made yet another application, causing his mother to waste valuable time and energy fighting a legal battle with his doctors – time she should have been using to find him somewhere stable to live.

In my view, the only possible description of a lot of what occurs in the public mental health and disability systems is *systems abuse*: the use of bureaucratic and legal systems to deny vulnerable people agency and punish them for not fully cooperating with their doctors' demands. Of course there are the #notallpsychiatrists caveats. But in my own twelve-month experience the exceptions were rare enough to prove the rule. It was remarkable how much a humane psychiatrist could improve the experiences of people living under involuntary treatment orders. Invariably, these (rare) doctors were better able to educate their patients and observe "insight," allowing patients to express frustrations without punishing them. But such doctors existed *despite* the systems they worked in, not because of them. From what I could tell, the systems also did a very poor job of supporting their own staff, including their doctors, whose standard shifts are often twelve hours long, and who – even before Covid-19 – were routinely required to work truly ridiculous hours. Doctors are, ironically, at much-elevated risk of suicide themselves. These systems are less about treatment and wellness for public mental health patients and disability clients than they are about maintaining a sense of controlled order for the rest of us.

I'm not for a moment suggesting that schizophrenia and other mental illnesses aren't difficult to treat. But it's hard to accept that we're making even adequate use of the abundant collective resources available to us, given that Australia is among the richest handful of states on the planet (on a per capita basis). Even if patients do need to be detained and force-injected, can't it be done with at least a modicum of humanity?

Krasnostein observes that "approximately 3189 people presented at the Austin Health emergency department for mental health issues" in 2018–19. I was one of them, taken there with significant "suicidal ideation." I'd never been suicidal before and haven't since. I was ultimately diagnosed with an "adjustment disorder," which apparently can be triggered by stress. I've made sure I haven't worked as hard as I was working in 2018. Melbourne's mental health system is light years ahead of those in Katherine (where I was living at the time), Darwin or Adelaide (where I now live). Still, as Krasnostein convincingly argues, it's far from what it should be. Emergency departments seem designed to erode the mental health of patients (by preventing them from sleeping) and staff. The secure psychiatric unit I found myself in for a few nights keeps people alive, mainly by frequent surveillance and the absence of hanging points, but it also seems designed to enhance depression. What helped me enormously was a four-week rent-free stay in a Prevention and Recovery Care (PARC) service house in Heidelberg Heights. Staffed round-the-clock by qualified mental health workers, the PARC house looks like an ordinary (if large) suburban house from the outside. Inside, ordinary people spend valuable weeks in the company of others, cooking, talking and recovering.

But outside the PARC houses – there really should be a lot more of them – society at large is being transformed into a gigantic factory for the production of mental illness. Stable housing is now practically impossible for a large and growing segment to come by. Employment standards and conditions in the private sector are worsening. Means-tested barriers to basic social security are fortified by remarkably complex bureaucratic requirements which cause many to simply give up.

The factory analogy seems confirmed by the apparent lack of any interest in prevention and early intervention. My partner, a social worker, has spent the last six months trying in vain to refer one of her clients – a teenage boy with classic signs of early psychosis – into a Headspace program which is funded on the basis that it provides "outreach" to its clients' homes. She knows what the current research says about the importance of getting teenagers quickly into treatment as soon as psychosis presents: in the most hopeful cases, early treatment can prevent a diagnosis of schizophrenia and a lifetime of inpatient stays in the adult public mental health system. Despite its "outreach" component, Headspace – the federal government's flagship youth mental health service – has required this boy to present to its offices, "to demonstrate a commitment to therapy." After multiple, confusing "intake" conversations at Headspace, during which he was asked the same questions over and over again, he told my partner he didn't want to pursue the referral. His future is not bright.

Another teenage boy has already been to court on multiple occasions for very serious domestic violence incidents. In and out of custody, he's also begun to say some very strange things, suggestive of psychosis. He says he doesn't want to hurt the people he loves, but recognises that he'll probably continue to do so unless he gets help. The system's only response so far, despite Herculean efforts by his lawyer (not me) and the youth court to have him referred to appropriate services, has been to arrest him and incarcerate him. Police now routinely verbally abuse him and goad him into physical confrontation, so they can justify using force against him. Various funded services – both government and non-government – have said he's unsuitable for their assistance, or that their waiting lists are too long. In her essay, Krasnostein gives us a glimpse into his likely future, and the future for any women who get close to him.

Russell Marks

Janet McCalman

Now that I have retired and have my pension, I can confess that I have been there too and done that. In 1976 I was locked up in the closed ward at Royal Park Psychiatric Hospital and emerged from a horror movie of delirium to find myself in strange clothing, in a strange place with a lot of iron bedsteads, with a couple of old women trying to get into my bed.

I had been stripped of all personal possessions, including my watch. But as I came to, it was still a recognisably human place, and my fellow inmates, many unable to speak, became less frightening once we were in the vast day room. Some were just crying. One old woman was visited by a man – perhaps her husband, perhaps her brother – while she babbled incoherently. He seemed utterly devoted.

The food was appalling, not that I had much appetite, and I learnt later that the budget per day per patient was 70 cents.

Then came the clinical assessment before twenty or so staff in a semicircle. I remember one particularly kindly and sympathetic face. They decided that I had recovered my wits, so I was sent to the open ward to rest for a few days.

There, it was quiet, and the only other patient was a young woman who was struggling with her identity and had admitted herself for a few days' breathing space. She could also discharge herself when she liked.

If I were suffering a similar psychotic episode today in one of our leading hospitals, I would be in a room of my own that is all white and has fluorescent lights on 24-7 so that I can be observed by video and prevented from self-harm.

When the Quakers and rational reformers got their hands on the prison system in Britain and its penal colonies, they railed against the lash and promoted reform of the soul above punishment of the body. This meant isolation, silence and surveillance.

In the solitary cells, prisoners convicted of secondary offences heard no sounds: all eating implements, buckets for wastes and water, and even the warders' feet were wrapped in cloth. You can see this at the panopticon at Port Arthur, where on the Sabbath prisoners attended church in a vertical coffin that cut them off from each other and directed their gaze at the preacher.

The reformers' "silent treatment" drove prisoners insane and shortened their lives, whereas flogging had not. Prisoners in the Millbank Penitentiary in London, the most modern in the land, begged to be transported to Van Diemen's Land and, if blessed to be chosen, collapsed on boarding in hysterics.

*

It is arguable that the biggest social policy failure of the post-war era has been the closing of the public psychiatric hospitals and the outsourcing of long-term care to families or the community. Certainly, we have looked away from a lot of deaths by suicide, by homicide and at police hands. But the narrative is that these hospitals were ugly, brutal places, best forgotten. And a critical architect of that narrative was the same Erving Goffman who wrote so brilliantly about stigma.

John C. Burnham, a distinguished historian of US psychiatry, commented that the closing of the asylums represented a perversion of liberalism. He recalled that there had been only one small study of the afterlife of those expelled into "freedom." This revealed that after five years, half of them were dead and the rest were being supported by people as poor as themselves.

But the rot had set in earlier in the United States, as the new liberalism in social policy that privileged the right to choose over the right to care had degraded the work of the asylums, which had once been committed to training people for work and independence but were now teaching them how to shop – the citizen as consumer, not worker.

Old Royal Park, many will remember from a trip along the freeway, had a small farm attached. The new "lunatic asylums" of the second half of the nineteenth century, lacking any psychotropic medications, had only physical restraint and occupational therapy, and high on that list was farm work and gardening, in the outdoors, with animals to tend and befriend. Animals and fresh air still work wonders and there is some effort to introduce animals into aged-care facilities.

A psychiatric nurse turned historian was looking at the Cambridge County Asylum in England, opened in 1858 and closed, like Royal Park, in the 1990s. When she examined the case records, she was hugely impressed by the quality of care in the nineteenth century. The wardsmen and women were locals from a long-depressed rural community who were suddenly offered good jobs, nice uniforms, dignity and security. She remarked that they did better at suicide watch, in a difficult building to police, than we do today.

And when Australia closed its asylums, with them went the therapeutic residential communities, the workshops and day centres, and of course the gardens and animals.

Like Sarah, I too read the pleas for mitigation in Supreme Court trials for grave crimes of violence. And I read the reports of the Coroner's Court of the preventable deaths in and out of care, of the suicides and of the overdoses. Nearly every perpetrator has a hideous childhood story of fragile parents struggling themselves with substance abuse, educational failure, inability to trust, wildly fluctuating moods and serious mental illness.

This knowledge helps me as an historian, for the convicts sent to Van Diemen's Land between 1803 and 1850 were similarly distinctive in that they were far more likely than their social peers to have lost one or both parents, exposing them as children to a life unprotected by a safe, functioning household. And those parents who were still living were often fragile breadwinners – alcoholic, unstable, unreliable.

Even worse for your life outcome, despite all the privations of transportation and penal servitude, was being born in a place that was especially dangerous for your mother – a place where the only work outside domestic service was in a public house or a brothel. That is, in a seaport like Liverpool, full of transients, prostitution and violence, where women and children were said to be "living in drunken savagery" in alleys and under bridges around the docks. Far better for life expectancy, marriage and children was to be born in rural Ireland and survive the Great Famine of the 1840s.

This will come as no surprise to those who work with criminal offenders, especially the young. And what has failed them is the household that is meant to protect and nurture them. And more often than not, that household has failed because the household a generation before, and a generation before that, has similarly failed. It is very hard to learn to trust, to give love and to be a good parent if you have no model.

But fragile households in turn are failed by a society that may pretend to care, but which will not invest emotionally and financially in sufficient help, in secure work, in affordable housing, education and training. Uncaring societies inflict structural violence on their most vulnerable members, and structural violence breaks minds and shortens lives.

The moral core of most societies draws on ethics about care for others. Churches and mosques and temples are obliged to care as a spiritual duty. But mostly they are ill-resourced. In 1601 England instituted the first secular welfare state, paid for by a tax (the poor rate), where the Old Poor Law acted as a "civic household" to the destitute, the friendless, the illegitimate, the sick and the homeless. And it worked until the mid-eighteenth century, when it was overwhelmed by demographic and economic change.

The welfare state, as it was reinvented in the mid-twentieth century, is intended to enable those without strong families to survive. It is an expression of a "duty of care" that is fundamental to all the world's great religions. Its remit, in Lord Beveridge's words, was to abolish "five giant evils: want, disease, ignorance, squalor, and idleness."

After the social-democratic high point post-war, this duty of care has been eroded: why should we subsidise the lazy and the stupid, the sick and the poor because of their bad habits? We need to grow wealth so that it will trickle down. And anyway, we are trampling on the right to choose your own destiny, even if you are unwell and without means and a home.

And so, when Jeff Kennett closed Royal Park in 1994, we didn't dump its residents to live in tents along the streets. We decanted them to the public housing towers, which today are our vertical, underserviced, lonely single wards for invalid pensioners, the majority with mental illness.

It's no longer as traumatic as it was in 1974, where distressed people wandered the streets of North Melbourne screaming for their pills, but too many still experience distress that in turn distresses their neighbours. And they are lonely, their daily lives consumed by their illness, as they will tell you in their first breath.

Those towers today are also incubators of mental illness in their newer, refugee population: suicide by jumping from a window, homicide while deranged, domestic violence and depression.

There was meant to be a proper support system for these outsourced patients in the 1990s, but there was never enough investment, the pay was too low, carers burnt out and people were left to medicate themselves.

Susan Reverby wrote a brilliant history of nursing in America called *Ordered to Care*, arguing that the dilemma of American nursing is that they are ordered to care in a society that refuses to value caring. And that's the rub.

By the time this letter is published we will know the result of the election. Anthony Albanese has committed to a "care-led recovery." This is our largest growing sector of the workforce and if we want proper aged care, childcare and mental healthcare, we need to value the carers. Few of the journalists and pundits seem to take this seriously: it lacks "vision" and is too small a target; surely it's unaffordable. They really don't get it.

Like global warming, the science is in on the effects of toxic stress in utero and early life. We know what to do for children and struggling parents to break the chain of intergenerational trauma and illness. It requires holding families together, not breaking them except in extremis, and intensive work building language skills, emotional resilience and personal capacity. It needs love and play, laughter and fun. It needs affordable housing and social infrastructure. And to do that we need well-paid, properly supported and trained carers of all kinds.

And it even makes economic sense. The think-tank Per Capita finds that the impact on GDP of the NDIS – the one the Morrison government considered too expensive – has an economic multiplier effect (conservatively estimated) of around 2.25. Currently it employs 270,000 people in over twenty occupations: that's a lot of jobs. In the great pandemic lockdown year of 2020–21, the NDIS made an economic contribution of around $52.4 billion to the nation. Improved mental and aged healthcare investments contribute likewise.

Even better, there would be less suffering and more happiness. There is no excuse any longer: our mutual care system from cradle to grave is the best investment we can make in our future as a society.

Janet McCalman

Nicola Redhouse

Cracks, walls, gaps, "acts of splitting," "living in old houses," "'ha-ha' walls" providing "an invisible divide," "cottages burnt to the ground," the enduring problem of housing, of how to "contain," how to "connect" – these are among the phrases I found myself noting repeatedly in Sarah Krasnostein's astute Quarterly Essay, which conjures a mental health system whose borders repeatedly collapse, open up, fall down; a system that cannot maintain a holding function, that buckles under the pain of its society.

Though Krasnostein writes that the "body politic cannot fit in a therapist's room," her essay develops into a fine attempt to bring it in, to comprehend what exactly is behind the breaks and gaps and disconnections. The work she does in this essay to get to the heart of our broken system accords with the techniques used in the field of socioanalysis, which attempts to understand the collective unconscious "phantasies" of a group as socially induced phenomena: that the behavioural dynamics of the group, its defences and dysfunctions, come about because the individuals within it have taken in a shared social experience.

In the context of a nation, according to socioanalytic thinking, it follows that the cultural and social responses we put into place (policies, laws, language uses, etc.) can be read as collective defences against our country's earliest traumas. Krasnostein parses these responses thoroughly.

For Australia, the "group as a whole" that Krasnostein details is a society built upon a significant early trauma: two "enormous acts of splitting: transportation and terra nullius." Such traumas, when they aren't properly mourned, are, according to Turkish Cypriot psychiatrist Vamık D. Volkan, unconsciously passed on to the next generation, "to complete these unfinished psychological processes." Volkan calls this the "chosen trauma."

Much like Krasnostein, I don't find it surprising, then, that as a nation we perpetuate shame, humiliation and dehumanisation in many of our health systems;

that we transform the seeking of asylum into something to be punished. Jon Jureidini, for example, taking a socioanalytic perspective, believes that our punitive asylum-seeker policies reflect our earliest identification as a remote island with "uncommon control over its borders," he writes in "Perverse asylum," a quality of isolation that has given rise to a "national characteristic of giving greater priority to the many than the weak and vulnerable."

Nor do I find it surprising that a nation established through force, by way of a colony centred on punishment, has, according to the *Australian Journal of Human Rights*, a "public mental health system ... skewed towards harmful and controlling forms of care."

And it is also unsurprising to see that the vulnerable describe their experiences in these systems as riddled with the same sicknesses as those of the nation's earliest life. To see, for example, in Victoria Legal Aid's *Your Story, Your Say* project – which "supported people with experience of mental health issues and services to tell their stories to the Royal Commission into Victoria's Mental Health System" – repeated themes of "distress, stigma and discrimination," of relationships "based on power and control" in mental health facilities.

All of this is only surprising if you maintain a position of denial; if you contend that who we have become has nothing to do with our earliest relationships, national or individual, and more significantly our earliest traumas.

Jenny Smith writes about the ways Australia's "chosen trauma" has played out in our treatment of asylum seekers, and makes a point central to the work of socioanalysis: that healing within a group involves leadership that can adopt what psychoanalyst and object-relations theorist Melanie Klein called the "depressive position": we must be "able to hold the 'good' desire to right the wrongs of the past," Smith writes, "and the 'bad' feelings of guilt and shame associated with what caused such trauma in the first place." Reparation depends on this capacity.

What will this take in the mental health sector? Krasnostein covers comprehensively various aspects of systemic change that need to come into play, and that the recent Victorian Royal Commission points towards. I can only add support to these.

At both a societal and an individual level, the work of repair needs time. I have written, in *The Age*, about the inadequacy of the Medicare-funded allocation of sessions for psychological treatment for developing what we know to be the central feature of good psychological care: the therapeutic alliance. Krasnostein highlights this inadequacy throughout her essay. Eliza's story conveys an experience of "insufficient time" with doctors, of hospital admissions where only "surface" behaviours were addressed.

The work of repair needs connections that foster trust. In Rebecca's story, we hear of incarcerations instead of trauma-informed care that would develop "close and continuing relationships, especially with clinicians." Time allows relationships to develop. Rationalism and consumerism threaten the necessary trust for effective psychological care. Hannah Piterman writes in her essay "Have we abandoned the patient?": "Without trust there is no clinical relationship and without a clinical relationship there can be no creative enterprise."

It will take a degree of de-medicalising of mental health, in recognition of the lasting value of working through trauma, balanced with the knowledge that, as Krasnostein demonstrates in canvassing the Verdins principles, the medicalisation of mental illness is sometimes required for appropriate legal outcomes.

It will take deep engagement at the level of thought and culture – the kind of deep engagement that socioanalytic dialogue gives rise to. It will take, as Krasnostein shows through the story of Daylia May Brown, a shift in ideology from one that places the burden of responsibility entirely on the individual to one that understands that people, like Krasnostein's interviewee Eliza, are the products of psycho-social experiences beyond their control. As Krasnostein notes: "one-quarter of all people admitted to acute mental health services are homeless prior to admission and most are discharged back into homelessness." She tells us that childhood trauma is a key driver of chronic homelessness, that adults who frequently experience racism are almost five times more likely to experience poor mental health.

We know from a wide field of research in psychology and neuroscience that how we interact with others and how we encounter the world is shaped, without our conscious awareness of it, by experiences we have early in life, both relational and material. So much of the aetiology of mental illness is beyond the individual's control. A model of healthcare that frames mental illness as the sole result of conscious individual life choices seems to serve the goals of a market-driven economy, but in fact we cannot afford to deny the connections that run between individuals and the worlds within which they exist, neither financially nor morally.

And while housing, jobs and affordable ongoing treatment are essential to improving outcomes, as Krasnostein points out, increased funding is not all that's needed. A deeper social shift is required – one that recognises the values of the relational experience, that closes the gaps not only materially but experientially.

Hannah Piterman writes that pharmacological solutions reflect a consumeristic accommodation of mental illness that is cost-effective and formulaic, but reflects "[an] omnipotent phantasy that has no place for illness, vulnerability and dependence. While the consumer is being served, the patient is being discarded and in some cases destroyed by a culture that discounts human experience and human suffering."

Similarly, Burkard Sievers notes of his work with organisations striving for greater market profitability that: "In face of the on-going struggle for excellence, growth and survival and the attempt to gain greater market shares, there seems to be almost no capacity for the depressive position and its anxieties ... no space for the experience of guilt, the desire for love, mourning or reparation."

We need to develop this capacity as a society not only for feeling, but for thinking. "Because being empathic and decent is demanding and potentially painful, we are all subject to retreating from it, both individually and as societies," writes Jureidini. As W. Gordon Lawrence notes in *Tongued with Fire*, when individuals regard "knowing" as too painful they "destroy, in various degrees, the very process of thinking that would put them in touch with reality." Socioanalysis proposes that this same mechanism occurs in a group, which enters a socially induced state of, as Sievers suggests, "totalitarian thinking."

Jureidini writes: "a decent society is one in which the leaders maintain a collective attitude of depressive concern." Depressive concern involves being in touch with reality, seeing what is happening and taking it in. We need to find a way to hold our society's pain at all levels – personal, institutional, governmental – without looking away.

Krasnostein's essay goes a long way towards keeping it in our line of sight.

Nicola Redhouse

James Dunk

As a historian, I was pleased to find that Sarah Krasnostein's Quarterly Essay about vulnerability in Australia is, as she writes, "always about history." It moves deftly through the short history of European colonisation here – from the anxieties and afflictions of the penal colony to their long shadows, falling everywhere around us. She argues that the psychological processes of convict transportation and colonisation survived the penal colony in masculinist cultures that stigmatise mental illness and deter the ill from seeking help, leading to egregious outcomes, including the alarmingly high suicide rate that has been a consistent feature of Australian history.

In the essay's sustained reflection on the 2019 Royal Commission into Victoria's Mental Health System, there is refreshing historical depth, placing the Commission not only in the "shadow of the penal colony," but in the more recent history of proliferating public inquiries. These are only the latest in an endless string of inquiries, which is a striking and exhausting facet of the modern history of mental health and mental illness. Exhausting not only in hours spent asking, answering and transcribing questions, but emotionally or spiritually exhausting. Commissioner after commissioner expresses horror and disgust at bedding or bathing practices, at the lack of therapeutics, at the class or capability of keepers, at the state of rations or visitation policies or at the personality flaws of superintendents: at everything, in short, and at who could possibly have authorised or funded or built or managed such a wretched institution. For those of us who have spent time working with that history, we come sooner or later to wonder at the amnesia and self-righteousness of the commissioner, and of the dialectic. Why should anyone have ever expected anything to be otherwise?

Because things are forgotten, writes Krasnostein. Because it has been helpful to forget. She brings depth psychology to bear here. She writes of our shadow selves, and of splitting selves, tracking the difficult line between individual psychopathology and social malaise. Asylums and hospitals become vehicles for our projected anxieties, sites for carving out and keeping out the most difficult parts of ourselves by doing slow violence to some of the most vulnerable members of our society. For a time, these institutions were palaces that exhibited, on the outside, the mastery of enlightenment rationality and mastery over the mind. They robustly secured by walls and laws those minds that strayed from the enlightened ideal. The emergence of effective psycho-pharmaceuticals in the post-war years offered relief from the costs of maintaining such elaborate structures, which, through endless inquiries, also became focal, vocal points for discontent with the whole entangled mess of what mental illness does to humans, and what humans do to other humans. Many of those purpose-built palaces are now crumbling or being repurposed, and the social barriers they buttressed have become more nebulous, with selves and populations harder to demarcate. And yet the inquiries continue, because people are still suffering, and their suffering is still and always alarming. The inquiries are compulsive acts, writes Krasnostein, where past trauma is recklessly and endlessly acted out instead of recalled, experienced and healed. These are social defence mechanisms gone to stale, barren seed.

The other kind of history here is personal history, the lived experience that elicits such inquiries. A genuine development in that steady stream of scrutiny is that commissioners have slowly learned to listen properly to the cared-for – consumers, clients, patients, survivors of psychiatric services – as well as the experts charged with their care. And their experience is, often, breathtakingly crushing. Max Weber described the onslaught of an industrial bureaucracy that aimed to strip away traditional impulses and motivators (like emotion) from the rational work of government. Bureaucracy may be, as he suggested, an iron cage in which we are slowly imprisoning ourselves, but *Not Waving, Drowning* shows the more violent parts of the system, in three studies of lives torn apart by the state or, at least, while the state sat back and watched. A friend who works in health policy told me that if the mental health system was funded properly, Australia would be broke in a fortnight. But these costs must always be borne, and they are. They are borne by those like the woman Krasnostein calls Rebecca, who spent eighteen months in a carceral forensic mental health facility because the court could not make a ruling. The court could not make a ruling, even though the "offence" had been minor, because there was nowhere it could rule her to be placed. This is not metaphorical. There was literally no place for her to live safe from further, compounding trauma. Krasnostein remains with her story through the long months in which many people met to solve a problem of which they were aware, including one where eighteen stakeholders (itself a major development or minor miracle) could not find a way to care for Rebecca because she fell between their agencies and systems. Everyone there was responsible for her, writes Krasnostein, and therefore no one was. For all its failings, the penal colony was governed from the centre, a colonial governor accepting moral and legal responsibility for those who were mentally ill on behalf of the Crown and deploying a rudimentary bureaucratic apparatus to solve problems and, often, to care for those who suffered. Those who assume the past is a dark or darker place are often surprised to find in my book *Bedlam at Botany Bay* a close and interpersonal colony, where compassion and care emerged within a wider program of discipline and terror and dispossession.

After two hundred years of bullish bureaucracy, the iron cage is straining awfully, and beginning perhaps to buckle under the weight of its dissociative fictions. The inquirers themselves – the archetypal commissioners – may finally be beginning to remember, and not repeat only. The conclusions of the Royal Commission into Victoria's Mental Health System showed the commissioners were aware of the long, long history of policy and moral failure, and aware too that a dataset and list of recommendations could do little to alter it. Daunting amounts of money and time were needed: billions of dollars and a decade or more to be spent on systems change, according to a theory in which real improvements are produced by changed relations between things. Krasnostein is at pains to show that those systems relations are in fact human relations, just as the gaps they aim to fill are embodied – are agonisingly realised – in the experience of the most vulnerable among us. More remarkable still, the Victorian government accepted the recommendations in full, rather than dodging and dissimulating, and has begun to implement them. It is, however, important that the reformers are not, as the minister has said, building a new system from scratch. They necessarily build in the ashes of the former system; they must build lucidly from history and memory, looking to those with lived experience of the old system to be architects of the new one.

James Dunk

John Kuot

Sarah Krasnostein may not be a mental health specialist, but her essay provides a good outline of all types of mental health and their level of impact on individuals trying to navigate the system. As someone who has worked across the public service and community sectors, I think Sarah's essay brilliantly captures the many frustrations of consumers and people working in mental health. The stories of Eliza, Daylia and Rebecca are not unique; instead, they perfectly reflect the many years of community outcry about the failures of the system. While traditional assessments of the system often narrate the experiences of individuals without including their voices, this essay evokes systematic failures by giving the perspectives of highly resilient individuals. I was moved by Eliza's outline of what help should have looked like for her. She explains that housing, financial support and someone to speak with would have enabled her to overcome some of the challenges she faced. What makes this essay different is the utilisation of these accounts to portray a very broken system. All the stories demonstrate that the failures are not just within mental healthcare, but are broader. Reading Daylia's and Rebecca's stories, I was shocked that our justice system, most of the time, exacerbates patients' conditions without consideration. That Rebecca – and many others in need – are too readily placed in prison rather than looked after illustrates why the conversation in this essay raises a wider issue of community responsibility, which needs immediate attention and action.

John Kuot

Joo-Inn Chew

Sarah Krasnostein listens to one of the young women she introduces in *Not Waving, Drowning*, 21-year-old Eliza, "on two levels ... with the interest of the 42-year-old author of this essay, watching how Eliza embodies decades of evidence that the negative outcomes associated with BPD [borderline personality disorder] might be mediated ... with favourable environmental influences," and also "with the admiration of the distressed eighteen-year-old" part of herself, who had suffered relational trauma but "hadn't attained the insights Eliza has and was convinced ... that she never would."

Krasnostein's essay is potent and radical for a multitude of reasons – her poetic and erudite blending of storytelling and analysis, and her synthesising of history, psychiatry, criminology and psychoanalysis to grapple with this country's fragile colonial past, which has stigmatised the vulnerable, dispossessed and marginalised. Most powerful to me was her decision to situate herself in the narrative, to have "chosen my fear of that stigma over silence in the face of it." In doing so, she removes another brick in the illusory and damaging wall we have built to render as "Other" those who experience mental illness and psychological distress. She speaks, and shares the voices of others, to show that "We" are "They," and "They" are "Us" – in the future or the past, in ourselves or our loved ones – and that mental anguish, grief, trauma and psychiatric illness are intimate parts of what it is to be human. There is no shame in this. Normalising our own vulnerabilities fosters insight and empathy, the prerequisites for the cultural and systemic changes which are so direly needed.

Such a "radical choice" is not easy. I am a GP with a long history of working in mental health, including with refugees and asylum seekers, the LGBTIQ+ community and in the prison system. I recognise the weary frustration of the front-line clinicians Krasnostein interviewed, who band-aid daily the deep distress of their patients in a system and society which is failing them. Like so many of us, I have my own complex history, which shapes how I work with people who are traumatised, and then pathologised and othered on top of that. I know what it is like to reach a place where my psychological pain transforms into compassion and healing for myself and others, where it makes me more, not less.

There is something familiar about this territory, this radical choice. I came out as a lesbian decades ago. I know the danger and freedom of no longer hiding, of stepping into the world on my own terms. I see now that coming out as having "a mental health history" is just as hard, especially as a clinician, as coming out as queer was in the 1980s and 1990s – scary and risky, yet full of transformative power. Something done in my own way and time, but which also connects me to those who have made (or will make) their own radical choices. Over time, all these choices expand our collective view of who "We" are.

When I worked in a regional Victorian hospital as an intern, I admitted a young woman brought in by ambulance with fresh lacerations up and down her arms. I went through the steps as gently as I could, aware of her terror and despair. As I checked her pulse between the bloodied cuts, I felt an echo inside me. My arms ached in sympathy because under my work sleeves were long pale scars from my own self-harm a few years before. I said nothing about them, but gave her my best compassionate care. Back in the 1990s, BPD elicited hostility from many doctors and nurses. It was not unusual for people who had self-harmed to be left waiting until last in emergency, and to be called "attention-seeking," "manipulative" and "incurable"; there were even stories of people having their cuts sutured without anaesthetic to "teach them a lesson." I have never been diagnosed with BPD, but I knew how it felt to be in a vortex of pain, to try to cut an escape route through my own flesh. I tried to keep my scars hidden, especially early in my career, but if a colleague noticed I would tell a brief version of the truth – that I had been depressed as a teenager – and watch their triple-take at my category transgression. I was supposed to be a Normal – in fact, a Super Normal, a Dr God-Robot, invulnerable and always on the right side of the stethoscope.

Decades have passed since that time on the wards, and there are few of my cohort who remain untouched by grief, trauma or despair, few who do not have scars on our skin or in our hearts. Suffering is universal; so too is hope and the possibility of healing. In my work I have sat with people trapped in the long shadow of childhood abuse. I have looked after people who are fleeing torture and persecution, only to be detained and denied protection by our government. I have known patients for longer than I have known my own children, and then lost them to suicide. I have carried the stories of so many people struggling with anxiety and depression and psychosis, with trauma and shame and stigma, as carefully as I carry my own. Behind each wound, each addiction, each diagnosis is a person and a story, and beyond that a web of cultural and economic power which shapes everything, from the start people get in life, to how they express distress and whether they seek help, to how they are treated by front-line services and social institutions. Not everyone knows what it is like to feel safe and free in Australia. Every one of us can take stock of where we are in the web, how we use the power we have and how we recognise the common humanity of people around us. We can normalise our own vulnerabilities and use our power well. I thank Sarah Krasnostein for an essay which invites us to do just that.

Joo-Inn Chew

NOT WAVING, DROWNING

Alexandra Goldsworthy

Sarah Krasnostein offers a sobering account of our current predicament, writing with insight about our systemic failures as a society, to ourselves and our families. I found myself teary and despairing when Krasnostein posed the questions in the last paragraph: "What would happen if we became curious about the sources of our strangely ambivalent relationship to change? If we acknowledged the fact that our vulnerability is our greatest strength because it is the source of true connection?"

I am a psychiatrist relatively early in my career, but already suffer from burnout and compassion fatigue. It comes in waves, not dissimilar to grief. As Krasnostein captures so eloquently in her essay, this state of physical and emotional exhaustion involves a sense of reduced accomplishment, helplessness and despair, and is shared by doctors (particularly our under-appreciated general practitioners), psychologists and other front-line clinicians. The main risk factors for burnout include lack of control; an inability to influence decisions that affect your work; unclear job expectations; chronic discomfort with holding excessive risk; lack of support; feeling isolated; and work–life imbalance. Work – and intrusive thoughts about patients' risk – uses so much bandwidth that little energy remains for family and friends. In my private practice, I see a fortunate group of patients who have managed to get to the right place at the right time. But every day, my colleagues and I reluctantly decline countless referrals due to lack of capacity. There are simply not enough clinicians to keep panning water out of a sinking boat. Sarah has an impeccable understanding of the contribution of trauma to the mental health crisis that we are drowning in. My burnout and grief, and clearly Sarah's grief, are accompanied by disbelief that we, as a society, continue to allow such appalling neglect of all members of our society.

Affectionless psychopathy is a term coined by John Bowlby, a psychiatrist and psychoanalyst who researched attachment and the importance of a reliable and safe relationship with at least one primary caregiver for normal social and emotional development. It describes individuals who cannot exhibit care, concern or affection for other people. Bowlby theorised that this is a consequence of long-term emotional deprivation in early childhood parental care. Parenting is so very complicated, yet so very simple. Children need to feel loved consistently and unconditionally.

Additionally, if a parent strives to foster a sense of security (essential for physical and mental health and self-esteem), they should also protect the child from physical and mental harm; comfort the child when distressed; ensure the child feels valued; see and know the child; and support the child in exploring, being vulnerable, trying unfamiliar things and making true connections. If, in this instance, we replace the word "child" with the words "Australian people," and "parent" with "government," I would suggest that our society is suffering from extreme neglect and abuse, leading in the best case to an emotional failure to thrive, and in the worst case to collective existential crisis, rising suicide and homicide rates and escalating screams for help falling on ears that refuse to listen. Perhaps I should report our government (mandatory, of course) to child protection to try to help ourselves? Knowing, obviously, that nothing will be done.

In my practice, I encounter person after person who is so riddled with shame that it obliterates their capacity to be vulnerable and to open up to themselves and that which may help them. The root of this shame is a belief that the abuse they suffered or the poverty they grew up in or their lack of education was their fault. They do not see that it was instead a symptom of a systemically traumatised society, with no parent caring enough to offer a safe and secure place of being. This shame is perpetuated by the systemic negligent responses seen everywhere they turn, including in emergency departments, ranging from the comments of ill-informed and overworked clinicians to practices such as being locked in a room, shackled to a hospital trolley or shoved to the barren psychiatric ward at the back of the hospital, and not being able to access psychologists or psychiatrists in the community.

Years of underfunding of psychiatric services informed my own clinical training, in which the most important KPI (key performance indicator) was the rapid turnover of inpatients, who were often discharged prematurely to under-resourced community "support." There was little time for appropriate humane care or connection. Instead, reliance on biological psychiatry (usually medication) was all we could do with the time and resources allocated. I do not know a single colleague who feels we are doing an adequate job.

How do we build a healthier society when our "parent" repeatedly looks the other way; is neglectful and emotionally depriving; is even unable to put a roof over our head and food in our bellies? The responsibility for raising our society appears to have been left to individuals: teachers, doctors, nurses, lawyers, counsellors. We have all been "left holding the baby," fully knowing that the baby has no home or food or safety beyond the relatively brief time they spend in our purview.

Employment, housing, education and social justice are leading determinants, of course. More generous and humane welfare support for families, primary caregivers and children would make a huge difference in those vital early years, alleviating undue stress and allowing secure attachments to form in our vulnerable young. Child protection policies in Australia have failed repeatedly. We desperately need experts and those with lived experience to inform good policy; we also desperately need good policy to be properly implemented and funded.

But I often wonder what kind of shift could occur, in a collective sense, if our leaders (parents?) tried to be sensitive, warm and empathic. If they listened when we expressed our pain and sadness and fear — or at least responded without a smirk. If they provided a nurturing environment in which we could feel safe, contained and held. If the people of Australia felt loved, unconditionally, by those who govern, perhaps we might have a more secure and robust attachment to our society, and more compassion for each other and for our leaders. Perhaps, as Krasnostein so beautifully articulates, we might reap the benefits of both vulnerability and togetherness.

Something has to change. The "she'll be right" mentality is not cutting it.

WE R NOT OK. Thank you, Sarah, for writing so eloquently for us all.

Alexandra Goldsworthy

NOT WAVING, DROWNING

Sebastian Rosenberg

Sarah Krasnostein's powerful essay *Not Waving, Drowning* demonstrates the moribund state of Australia's mental healthcare "system." But to call our mental health system broken suggests that it was once whole. This couldn't be further from the truth. There has never been a genuine set of alternative mental health services in the community. Our current situation is akin to trying to put together pieces from different jigsaw puzzles.

Krasnostein first describes the terrible everyday experiences of individuals attempting to find help. The essay's three key case studies highlight the gaps and failures to which families and communities have unfortunately become accustomed. People struggle to find help, face delays in getting the right diagnosis or treatment and become very sick, isolated and at real risk of harm to self or others.

There is dissonance here. A rich country, Australia is regularly lauded as having one of the world's best health systems. And yet the stories of poor care, missing care or abuse in mental health are well known. They were documented in a report I was involved with back in 2005, entitled *Not for Service*. Prepared jointly by the Australian Human Rights Commission and (the organisation now known as) Mental Health Australia, the report's title denotes how the Victorian state mental health system categorised a troublesome patient seeking care – that person was classified as being "not for service."

Typically called consumers, people using mental health services have told their stories of continuing abuse and powerlessness to repeated parliamentary committees, statutory inquiries and royal commissions. There would surely be few areas of government activity more subject to formal inquiry than mental health. All this inquiring generates a blizzard of actions, recommendations and strategies – a plandemic. Yet mental health's share of the total health budget in Australia was 7.25 per cent in 1992–93, when the National Mental Health Strategy began, and in 2019–20 (the latest year available) it had hardly changed at 7.57 per cent.

If this were any other body part, there would be uproar about the abject failure of the health system. Perhaps this reflects the ongoing impact of stigma described in the essay.

But I think there's more to it. If you ask people with a mental illness, any type of mental illness, what they are most concerned about, they will typically prioritise secure housing, the capacity to earn a living and the social connections which make life worth living. Australia collects almost no specific data on the quality of life of people with a mental illness or whether the care they received helped them go home, find or keep a job, or improved their relationships. We are spending $11 billion each year on direct mental health services, but we know almost nothing about the merit of this spending. Is anybody getting better?

Without this information, as pointed out recently by the Productivity Commission, we are outcome-blind. We are vulnerable to a view that somehow people with a mental illness are not worth spending time or money on. This is stigma.

A scan of a map of Sydney Harbour will reveal that the body of water adjacent to the old Gladesville asylum is named Bedlam Bay – a legacy of colonial laws preventing the mentally ill from travelling the King's highways. Incoming patients were instead transported by boats, disembarking at Bedlam Point.

Krasnostein writes that Australia's mental health system is broken and in need of fundamental reform. She quotes one of the people with a mental illness as saying, "You can't heal in the environment that made you sick." Some consumers certainly report feeling that the services or hospitals they visit are toxic environments rather than places of healing. But all those reports and inquiries document not only the voice of consumers, but also the well-intentioned health professionals describing "iatrogenic harm" – the inadvertent harm caused by treatment. Health professionals themselves recognise they cannot deliver quality mental healthcare in existing settings.

When the old mental asylums in Australia closed, two replacement institutions emerged: the psychiatric wards of our public hospitals and jails. Of the $6.6 billion spent by the states and territories, around 80 per cent would be directed towards hospital-based mental healthcare – inpatient and outpatient. Australia has never really funded mental healthcare outside of hospitals, in people's homes or in the community. While people with mental illness are now permitted to use the King's roads, those roads all lead to our choked emergency departments. And a 2019 report by St Vincent's found that 40 per cent of all Australian prisoners have a mental illness.

I suggest that Australia's mental health system is not broken. It has never been built.

The federal government funds Medicare, which is primarily designed to provide GP and psychology services to people with anxiety and depression. The states deal with rarer mental illnesses, such as schizophrenia and bipolar disorder, through public hospital care. Two different funders for two different client groups. So what happens to the person with schizophrenia when they are well? How is their physical health managed? What about a person with severe anxiety? Where should they go for help if their condition improves or deteriorates?

The result of this fragmentation is that if you have a mental illness that is too difficult or complicated for your local GP or psychologist, Australians have almost no choice but to go to the accident and emergency department of their local public hospital to seek assistance. Key opportunities to provide care in other settings are missed, leaving only the most expensive and often traumatic option of going to hospital. Other illnesses focus on early intervention – addressing the cancerous lump before it grows larger. In mental health, if your lump isn't large enough you get sent home until it grows. And that's if you get seen at all – not assured by any means, as Krasnostein reports in the essay.

A person with more complex mental health needs will often require a team. Take, for example, a young person with an eating disorder. Their care is likely to benefit from a team including a GP, a nurse, a psychologist, a psychiatrist, a dietician, a peer worker and other allied health workers (for example, to keep the person connected to their education or employment).

But mental healthcare in Australia is based on people going to see health professionals who work solo, typically charging considerable out-of-pocket costs, rarely coordinated to work in teams. Recent Medicare funding enabling this young person to see the same practitioner forty times may not be enough to address their complex problems. Only one in three Medicare mental health patients were new in 2019–20. Most are repeat customers, forced to continue to seek help because they did not get the right help the first time.

Technology can help provide care, monitor the impact of that care on a person's wellbeing and help coordinate the team (through shared records, etc.), but investments here are negligible.

One of the most famous mental health services in the world is in Trieste, Italy. There, psychiatrists led a revolution against acute, locked, hospital care in favour of a new model of multidisciplinary health and social care in the community. Australia's psychiatrists and other health professionals seem too content with the status quo – with hospital-based care or the certainty of Medicare fee-for-service payments – to contemplate any such revolution here. In Trieste they say, "Da vicino, nessuno e normale" – up close, nobody is normal. And you get a sense of this as you walk the streets there. With some subsidised arrangements for employment, a person with a mental illness might be driving your bus, making your (excellent) coffee or cooking your lunch. Their mental health needs can be met on the high street near where they live, or even in their own home. It is an irony that Australia pioneered the concept of hospital in the home with mental health decades ago. Home visits are rare now (even pre-Covid). People get phoned, not visited.

The government can play a lead role in enhancing the social democratic reflexes of Australian society, as Krasnostein puts it. This is because effective mental healthcare should not focus on the health system. It should focus on employment and housing. Given that 75 per cent of all mental illnesses manifest before the age of twenty-five, it should focus on education. Change at this level is way beyond tinkering. It needs much more than a few new beds here, another hotline there or some new, comfy beanbags for the local Headspace.

Central to this more fundamental reform is to finally recognise psycho-social care as a vibrant and respected partner to clinical care. Psycho-social services have never accounted for more than about 8 per cent of all mental health spending, but they provide vital counselling services, accommodation support, self-help, support for families, carers and peers, as well as assistance with employment, education and recreation. These services barely exist, leaving mental healthcare stuck as just a medical problem.

Addressing this imbalance, as well as ensuring access to quality clinical care, would give people a fair chance to live well in the community. And this was the point of deinstitutionalisation. Not just to swap one institution for another.

The 2022 federal budget, announced as Krasnostein's essay appeared, smeared some new funding across myriad, often time-limited programs and services. Links to state spending, even the significant new spending in Victoria arising from its royal commission, are unclear or missing. New funding cannot be wasted by perpetuating fragmentation. We must stop pouring more oil into this leaky engine.

Thirty years on from Australia's first national mental health strategy, Krasnostein's essay demonstrates the scale and urgency of the fundamental reform still required.

Sebastian Rosenberg

Sarah Krasnostein

A few weeks after I finished writing Quarterly Essay 85, the federal budget was handed down, a federal election was called and punitive populist politicking – ever-present in the nation's sphere of accepted political discourse – was turned up to eleven. Like the emotional experience of researching the case studies and figures in my essay, these events brought further examples of how it is possible – ironically – to be unsurprised by human decision-making that shocks the conscience.

In the lead-up to the election, we saw the two major parties haemorrhage finite time on the specious need to "turn back the boats" and the concocted debate over the fundamental human dignity of trans people. We heard deafening silence, however, when it comes to the actual, enormous and urgent need to significantly invest (money, time, attention, effort, training) in the mental health of Australians generally, and already-marginalised groups specifically. Given that both parties have commissioned research about not only the scope of the mental health catastrophe in this country, but also the ways in which Othering – in all its forms – compounds and causes mental illness, these hypocrisies signify something that has not yet been psychologically mastered, something ill at ease with itself and intentionally self-deluded, as Theodor Adorno put it in the context of post-war Germany.

Despite the slick marketing labels – "Guaranteeing the essentials" and "Modernising the mental health system" – this was a federal budget that did neither of these things. As Sebastian Rosenberg put it in his thoughtful response to my essay: "The 2022 federal budget ... smeared some new funding across myriad, often time-limited programs and services. Links to state spending ... are unclear or missing. New funding cannot be wasted by perpetuating fragmentation. We must stop pouring more oil into this leaky engine."

It struck me that a shared theme across the correspondence is that of moral injury. This can be understood as the eviscerating betrayal of one's conscience when one is compelled to operate within a system that discourages values such as fairness, effectiveness, compassion and justice. "I am a psychiatrist relatively early in my career," Alexandra Goldsworthy movingly wrote, "but already suffer from burnout and compassion fatigue. It comes in waves, not dissimilar to grief ... this grief is a state of physical and emotional exhaustion involving a sense of reduced accomplishment, helplessness and despair."

I am grateful for this intimate insight. I had previously been aware of the ways in which our mental health care system is itself iatrogenic, causing harm to patients, carers and families through myriad institutional failings. I had also been aware of the prevalence of secondary trauma among clinicians, lawyers and police who work in these systems. While related to those harms, moral injury is, however, an independent, additional wounding.

Goldsworthy continued: "Years of underfunding of psychiatric services informed my own clinical training, in which the most important KPI was the rapid turnover of inpatients, who were often discharged prematurely to under-resourced community 'support' ... I do not know a single colleague who feels we are doing an adequate job."

Relatedly, Janet McCalman, in her finely synthesised reply, stated that "the dilemma of American nursing is that they are ordered to care in a society that refuses to value caring. And that's the rub." Joo-Inn Chew writes – beautifully, powerfully – of recognising "the weary frustration of the front-line clinicians [interviewed in the essay] who band-aid daily the deep distress of their patients in a system and society which is failing them." This theme of moral injury is also present in Russell Marks' revelatory interrogation of authority at the intersection of our mental health and legal systems: "In my view, the only possible description of a lot of what occurs in the public mental health and disability systems is *systems abuse*: the use of bureaucratic and legal systems to deny vulnerable people agency ... the systems also did a very poor job of supporting their own staff."

"We don't value the caring professions," one woman – an academic and a mother with lived experience of trying to secure effective psychiatric care for herself and her two children – told me when I was researching the essay. Her acuity gave me goosebumps. The mental health system was already understaffed before the workforce problems caused by Covid-19. We underestimate the prevalence and impact of moral injury among those in the caretaking professions at our collective peril. I am grateful to the correspondents for bringing this to my attention.

The correspondence also speaks, from different valuable angles, to the ways in which personal wounds affect group psychology and therefore political behaviour: what we will see, what we will tolerate, what we will participate in. "So much of our public expenditure is, in the old parlance of health bureaucracy, sending ambulances to wait at the bottom of the cliff," wrote Rick Morton, with characteristic insight. "It has become fashionable to frame these moral truths in the language of ideology. Unemployment benefits, according to some, are not meant to be 'easy' to live on because then people might actually manage to live on them. But if you're not inclined to believe the bleeding hearts, ask the hard-headed economists and researchers at the Productivity Commission."

Jennifer Doggett – to whom I have long been thankful for her clear-sighted analyses of health policy and practice – wrote: "It seems that mental illness is a mirror which reflects back to the viewer their existing concerns, anxieties and ideologies. In this way it reinforces the ideologies and worldviews which divide us, making it difficult to work together to develop a common response."

We are united in the fears and emotional reactivity that separate us. Luckily, facts do not care about ideology. Countless publicly funded fact-finding missions have provided us with a wealth of data about the causative and compounding impacts on poor mental health of stigma and discrimination, housing insecurity, job insecurity, imprisonment, lack of early intervention, care, treatment and support, domestic violence, and childhood abuse and emotional neglect.

"What is maddening about all of this," Morton continued, "is that we have arranged our collective social mind to hide away the uncomfortable truths about mental illness." While it is true, then, that facts don't care about ideology, facts alone do not move the world. Again, Morton: "It feels too big, I suppose, to stare down the role of poverty; family dysfunction; the harsh illogic of the justice system; chronic pain and physical ailments; the stress of being any kind of 'other'; physical or emotional traumas; and government systems meant … to provide support but which come booby-trapped by negligence or, worse, malicious intent."

In what has gone unsaid and unseen and unchallenged, the final weeks of campaigning and media coverage evoked in me an uncanny dread. The familiar, and pathological, political patterns continue: investing public money in public inquiries only to ignore or cherry-pick their findings; politicians refusing to model the behaviours they purportedly expect from sectors and services; and the deliberate use of already-vulnerable groups as political footballs, despite government-funded evidence that stigmatisation and othering increase the risk of suicide.

Our leaders persist in their delusive aversion to enacting the solutions we are by now well informed about. Nicola Redhouse eloquently describes this political and institutional dysregulation as "a mental health system whose borders repeatedly collapse, open up, fall down; a system that cannot maintain a holding function, that buckles under the pain of its society." Too much of the electorate – and the media, whose role is to hold power to account – also have a hand in this. A critical mass continues to "defend themselves against the progress of the treatment," in Freud's words.

Redhouse rightfully located this main concern of the essay within the field of socioanalysis, "which attempts to understand the collective unconscious 'phantasies' of a group as socially induced phenomena: that the behavioural dynamics of the group, its defences and dysfunctions, come about because the individuals within it have taken in a shared social experience." I am thankful for her observations, especially considering the impact that two texts had on my thinking: Freud's "Group Psychology and the Analysis of the Ego" (1921) and Adorno's "The Meaning of Working Through the Past" (1959), both masterful interrogations of the ways in which individual psychology is an inevitable aspect of social psychology.

This leads to the last theme I'd like to highlight from the correspondence, that of the still-determinative influences of our national history – "from the anxieties and afflictions of the penal colony to their long shadows, falling everywhere around us," as James Dunk elegantly put it. I am grateful to Dunk and Rosenberg for tracing – from different but equally illuminating perspectives – not just our mental health care system's failure to thrive since, at the very least, the late colonial period, but its failure (our failure) to adapt to the reality of social needs.

In addressing the mental health crisis, there is a vital, reparative role to be played by our historians, our storytellers, our artists, our educators, our readers and everyone who can find it within themselves to listen to what Aboriginal community-controlled organisations have been telling us for decades. These are the people whose lives are devoted to practices of truly knowing, and properly grieving, the past. That is the precondition for not repeating its violence. Personally and politically, we cannot cope with what has not been made conscious. "This is the social-psychological relevance of talk about an unmastered past," Adorno wrote over sixty years ago.

"Commissioner after commissioner expresses horror and disgust at bedding or bathing practices," Dunk wrote, about the repetitions of that past, "at the lack of therapeutics, at the class or capability of keepers, at the state of rations or visitation policies or at the personality flaws of superintendents … For those of us who have spent time working with that history, we come sooner or later to wonder at the amnesia and self-righteousness of the commissioner, and of the dialectic. Why should anyone have ever expected anything to be otherwise? Because things are forgotten … Because it has been helpful to forget." Now, however, "[a]fter two hundred years of bullish bureaucracy, the iron cage is straining awfully, and beginning perhaps to buckle under the weight of its dissociative fictions."

That collapsing of borders described earlier by Redhouse is also inherent to apophenia – the human tendency to perceive a connection or meaningful pattern between unrelated things. This is a characteristic of certain mental illnesses as well as of all artistic endeavour, rational thought and perhaps the quality of empathy itself. Which is all to say that even though I have gone on to new assignments, I am still thinking about the people at the heart of my essay, and still finding greater understanding in unexpected places.

I recently finished a deceptively slender book by Ross Gibson titled *Seven Versions of an Australian Badland* (UQP, 2002), which interrogates white mythologies of Queensland's landscape. Gibson defines myth as "a popular story that highlights contradictions which a community feels compelled to resolve narratively rather than rationally, so that citizens can get on living." I think about our shared grammar of evasion within that framework: *She'll be right. Toughen up. Pretty ordinary. Border Force. Religious discrimination. Guaranteeing the essentials. Modernising the mental health system.* "Myths help us live with contradictions," Gibson wrote, "whereas histories help us analyse persistent contradictions so that we might avoid being lulled and ruled by the myths that we use to console and enable ourselves."

While we desire our myths, we need our histories, Gibson tells us. "The histories of most nations founded on violence suggest that an inability or refusal to acknowledge the past will produce evermore confusing and distressing symptoms in the body politic," he writes. "In the wishful shelter of ignorance or amnesia, an abiding melancholy tends to creep into the populace. Or equally disabling, the society can succumb to a paranoid urge to expunge all dissenting persons and memories." As happens in the counselling room, techniques of national insight and grieving are required "so that the denials might cease, so that guilt and threat might be 'lived out', and citizens might start to earn some kind of worldly wisdom, scars and all."

Without this unflinching confrontation with the reality of our history, future generations will "continue to live in the shadow of denial and repression of events that cannot be undone by acts of forgetting," as Margarete and Alexander Mitscherlich wrote decades ago. These are not simply acts of remembering. They are also acts of seeing – health and justice and educational and housing outcomes in real time, this minute; a lived history, as Sheree Lowe, executive director of the Victorian Aboriginal Controlled Community Health Organisation's Aboriginal Social and Emotional Wellbeing Centre, put it in the essay.

You are reading this with knowledge of the election's outcome, which I lack at the time of writing this. But the weeks of campaigning have showcased the continued normalisation of punitive paranoias, which indicate that the nation has not yet earned the label "post-colonial" or "post-traumatic." "The past will have been worked through only when the causes of what happened then have been eliminated," Adorno wrote. "Only because the causes continue to exist does the captivating spell of the past remain to this day unbroken."

Favourable or otherwise, serious engagement with one's work is a gift. Engagement that understands the work in the way one intended is exceptional. Goldsworthy's use of the following analogy to trace the line from the interior to the communal was a bullseye; she hit the heart of the matter: "We desperately need experts and those with lived experience to inform good policy; we also desperately need good policy to be properly implemented and funded. But I often wonder what kind of shift could occur, in a collective sense, if our leaders (parents?) tried to be sensitive, warm and empathic ... If the people of Australia felt loved, unconditionally, by those who govern, perhaps we might have a more secure and robust attachment to our society, and more compassion for each other and for our leaders."

This is the "wider issue," as Australian Fulbright scholar and correspondent John Kuot put it, and its acuity reminded me of something Kuot told me in an interview for the essay, when he emphasised the foundational importance of belonging in the context of the mental health of migrants and asylum seekers: "What people fail to understand is in the environment they've come to, their background experiences might not be the biggest trauma – there might be a new trauma. There are the challenges of isolation where you feel so different all the time and your only survival mechanism is code-switching. You have to be two people in one in almost every environment, and you can never be consistently one. That presents challenges for any young person, cognitively. There's only so much a brain can take ... If you live in the same household and different standards are applied, you will never feel like you belong in that home."

I have been heartened by, and learnt much from, each of the responses printed here and those I received directly. They have enlarged my understanding of the topic. And they have strengthened my conviction that we must look broadly at the external landscape, and deeply into our interior ones, because there are no "unchlorinated areas of the pool" when it comes to our social and emotional health and wellbeing.

Finally, I am especially grateful to Marks, Chew, McCalman, Morton, Redhouse and Goldsworthy – and those readers who contacted me directly – for their willingness to normalise their personal mental health experiences and share their vulnerability in the face of the pervasive stigma in this country. Those radical acts – "scary and risky, yet full of transformative power," in Chew's words – have expanded my optimism that harms relationally created can be relationally solved.

Sarah Krasnostein

Joo-Inn Chew works in general practice and refugee health in Canberra. She has worked in regional Victoria, in hospitals and in prison medicine. Her writing has featured in publications including Black Inc.'s *Growing Up* series and *Sunday Magazine*. She edited *Heart Murmurs: Stories by Canberra GPs*.

Jennifer Doggett is a fellow of the Centre for Policy Development and a consultant working in the health sector for a number of professional, industry and consumer groups. She is an editor at Croakey Health Media and a contributor to debates on health issues in the media and policy forums.

James Dunk lives and writes on Wangal Country in Sydney's inner west. He works as a historian at the University of Sydney, exploring how psychology and mental health have encountered the planetary environment. His first book, *Bedlam at Botany Bay*, won the Australian History Prize at the 2020 New South Wales Premier's History Awards.

Alexandra Goldsworthy is a psychiatrist who works in a private practice in Adelaide.

Sarah Krasnostein is the multi-award-winning author of *The Trauma Cleaner*, *The Believer* and the Quarterly Essay *Not Waving, Drowning*. Her writing has appeared in magazines and journals in Australia, the United Kingdom and America. She holds a doctorate in criminal law.

John Kuot has worked as a youth officer at the Victorian youth prison in Parkville, for the Victorian Department of Premier and Cabinet as an adviser, and in the private and community sectors. He was awarded a Fulbright Scholarship and is currently studying Economic Policy Management at Columbia University. He came to Australia as a refugee in 2004 and was co-founder of the youth-led charity organisation South Sudanese Australia Youth United.

Janet McCalman is known for her award-winning social histories *Struggletown* (1984), *Journeyings* (1993), *Sex and Suffering* (1998) and *Vandemonians* (2021). In 2020 she co-edited with Emma Dawson *What Happens Next? Reconstructing Australia after COVID-19*, and for over twenty years she taught interdisciplinary history and public health at the University of Melbourne.

Russell Marks is a criminal defence lawyer and an adjunct research fellow at La Trobe University. He writes for *The Monthly*, and is the author of *Black Lives, White Law: Locked Up and Locked Out in Australia* (forthcoming) and *Crime and Punishment: Offenders and Victims in a Broken Justice System*.

Rick Morton is the author of three non-fiction books, including the critically acclaimed, bestselling memoir *One Hundred Years of Dirt* and essays on love and mental illness in *My Year of Living Vulnerably*. He is the senior reporter at *The Saturday Paper*.

Nicola Redhouse is the Melbourne-based author of *Unlike the Heart: A Memoir of Brain and Mind* (UQP). Her writing has appeared in *Guardian Australia*, *The Monthly*, *The Australian*, *The Age* and *Best Australian Stories*.

Sebastian Rosenberg began at the Brain and Mind Centre in 2009, after studying history and public administration, then working in government and non-government agencies. He completed his PhD, "Is Anybody Getting Better: Accountability for Mental Health in Australia", in 2017, and has published widely in academic journals and other publications.

Hugh White is the author of *The China Choice* and *How to Defend Australia*, and of the acclaimed Quarterly Essays *Power Shift* and *Without America*. He is emeritus professor of strategic studies at ANU and was principal author of Australia's Defence White Paper 2000.

WANT THE LATEST FROM
QUARTERLY ESSAY?

**Subscribe to the Friends of Quarterly Essay
email newsletter to share in news, updates,
events and special offers.**

---

quarterlyessay.com.au/signup

QUARTERLY ESSAY
BACK ISSUES

BACK ISSUES: (Prices include GST, postage and handling within Australia.) *Grey indicates out of stock.*

- ☐ **QE 1** ($17.99) Robert Manne *In Denial*
- ☐ **QE 2** ($17.99) John Birmingham *Appeasing Jakarta*
- ☐ **QE 3** ($17.99) Guy Rundle *The Opportunist*
- ☐ **QE 4** ($17.99) Don Watson *Rabbit Syndrome*
- ☐ **QE 5** ($17.99) Mungo MacCallum *Girt By Sea*
- ☐ **QE 6** ($17.99) John Button *Beyond Belief*
- ☐ **QE 7** ($17.99) John Martinkus *Paradise Betrayed*
- ☐ **QE 8** ($17.99) Amanda Lohrey *Groundswell*
- ☐ **QE 9** ($17.99) Tim Flannery *Beautiful Lies*
- ☐ **QE 10** ($17.99) Gideon Haigh *Bad Company*
- ☐ **QE 11** ($17.99) Germaine Greer *Whitefella Jump Up*
- ☐ **QE 12** ($17.99) David Malouf *Made in England*
- ☐ **QE 13** ($17.99) Robert Manne with David Corlett *Sending Them Home*
- ☐ **QE 14** ($17.99) Paul McGeough *Mission Impossible*
- ☐ **QE 15** ($17.99) Margaret Simons *Latham's World*
- ☐ **QE 16** ($17.99) Raimond Gaita *Breach of Trust*
- ☐ **QE 17** ($17.99) John Hirst *'Kangaroo Court'*
- ☐ **QE 18** ($17.99) Gail Bell *The Worried Well*
- ☐ **QE 19** ($17.99) Judith Brett *Relaxed & Comfortable*
- ☐ **QE 20** ($17.99) John Birmingham *A Time for War*
- ☐ **QE 21** ($17.99) Clive Hamilton *What's Left?*
- ☐ **QE 22** ($17.99) Amanda Lohrey *Voting for Jesus*
- ☐ **QE 23** ($17.99) Inga Clendinnen *The History Question*
- ☐ **QE 24** ($17.99) Robyn Davidson *No Fixed Address*
- ☐ **QE 25** ($17.99) Peter Hartcher *Bipolar Nation*
- ☐ **QE 26** ($17.99) David Marr *His Master's Voice*
- ☐ **QE 27** ($17.99) Ian Lowe *Reaction Time*
- ☐ **QE 28** ($17.99) Judith Brett *Exit Right*
- ☐ **QE 29** ($17.99) Anne Manne *Love & Money*
- ☐ **QE 30** ($17.99) Paul Toohey *Last Drinks*
- ☐ **QE 31** ($17.99) Tim Flannery *Now or Never*
- ☐ **QE 32** ($17.99) Kate Jennings *American Revolution*
- ☐ **QE 33** ($17.99) Guy Pearse *Quarry Vision*
- ☐ **QE 34** ($17.99) Annabel Crabb *Stop at Nothing*
- ☐ **QE 35** ($17.99) Noel Pearson *Radical Hope*
- ☐ **QE 36** ($17.99) Mungo MacCallum *Australian Story*
- ☐ **QE 37** ($17.99) Waleed Aly *What's Right?*
- ☐ **QE 38** ($17.99) David Marr *Power Trip*
- ☐ **QE 39** ($17.99) Hugh White *Power Shift*
- ☐ **QE 40** ($17.99) George Megalogenis *Trivial Pursuit*
- ☐ **QE 41** ($17.99) David Malouf *The Happy Life*
- ☐ **QE 42** ($17.99) Judith Brett *Fair Share*

- ☐ **QE 43** ($17.99) Robert Manne *Bad News*
- ☐ **QE 44** ($17.99) Andrew Charlton *Man-Made World*
- ☐ **QE 45** ($17.99) Anna Krien *Us and Them*
- ☐ **QE 46** ($17.99) Laura Tingle *Great Expectations*
- ☐ **QE 47** ($17.99) David Marr *Political Animal*
- ☐ **QE 48** ($17.99) Tim Flannery *After the Future*
- ☐ **QE 49** ($17.99) Mark Latham *Not Dead Yet*
- ☐ **QE 50** ($17.99) Anna Goldsworthy *Unfinished Business*
- ☐ **QE 51** ($17.99) David Marr *The Prince*
- ☐ **QE 52** ($17.99) Linda Jaivin *Found in Translation*
- ☐ **QE 53** ($17.99) Paul Toohey *That Sinking Feeling*
- ☐ **QE 54** ($17.99) Andrew Charlton *Dragon's Tail*
- ☐ **QE 55** ($17.99) Noel Pearson *A Rightful Place*
- ☐ **QE 56** ($17.99) Guy Rundle *Clivosaurus*
- ☐ **QE 57** ($17.99) Karen Hitchcock *Dear Life*
- ☐ **QE 58** ($17.99) David Kilcullen *Blood Year*
- ☐ **QE 59** ($17.99) David Marr *Faction Man*
- ☐ **QE 60** ($17.99) Laura Tingle *Political Amnesia*
- ☐ **QE 61** ($17.99) George Megalogenis *Balancing Act*
- ☐ **QE 62** ($17.99) James Brown *Firing Line*
- ☐ **QE 63** ($17.99) Don Watson *Enemy Within*
- ☐ **QE 64** ($17.99) Stan Grant *The Australian Dream*
- ☐ **QE 65** ($17.99) David Marr *The White Queen*
- ☐ **QE 66** ($17.99) Anna Krien *The Long Goodbye*
- ☐ **QE 67** ($17.99) Benjamin Law *Moral Panic 101*
- ☐ **QE 68** ($17.99) Hugh White *Without America*
- ☐ **QE 69** ($17.99) Mark McKenna *Moment of Truth*
- ☐ **QE 70** ($17.99) Richard Denniss *Dead Right*
- ☐ **QE 71** ($17.99) Laura Tingle *Follow the Leader*
- ☐ **QE 72** ($17.99) Sebastian Smee *Net Loss*
- ☐ **QE 73** ($17.99) Rebecca Huntley *Australia Fair*
- ☐ **QE 74** ($17.99) Erik Jensen *The Prosperity Gospel*
- ☐ **QE 75** ($17.99) Annabel Crabb *Men at Work*
- ☐ **QE 76** ($17.99) Peter Hartcher *Red Flag*
- ☐ **QE 77** ($17.99) Margaret Simons *Cry Me a River*
- ☐ **QE 78** ($17.99) Judith Brett *The Coal Curse*
- ☐ **QE 79** ($17.99) Katharine Murphy *The End of Certainty*
- ☐ **QE 80** ($17.99) Laura Tingle *The High Road*
- ☐ **QE 81** ($17.99) Alan Finkel *Getting to Zero*
- ☐ **QE 82** ($17.99) George Megalogenis *Exit Strategy*
- ☐ **QE 83** ($24.99) Lech Blaine *Top Blokes*
- ☐ **QE 84** ($24.99) Jess Hill *The Reckoning*
- ☐ **QE 85** ($24.99) Sarah Krasnostein *Not Waving, Drowning*

Please include this form with delivery and payment details overleaf.
Back issues also available as eBooks at **quarterlyessay.com**

SUBSCRIBE TO RECEIVE
10% OFF THE COVER PRICE

☐ **ONE-YEAR PRINT AND
DIGITAL SUBSCRIPTION: $89.99**

- Print edition
- Home delivery
- Automatically renewing
- Full digital access to all past issues
- App for Android and iPhone users
- eBook files

DELIVERY AND PAYMENT DETAILS

DELIVERY DETAILS:

NAME:

ADDRESS:

EMAIL: PHONE:

PAYMENT DETAILS: Enclose a cheque/money order made out to Schwartz Books Pty Ltd.
Or debit my credit card (MasterCard, Visa and Amex accepted).
Freepost: Quarterly Essay, Reply Paid 90094, Collingwood VIC 3066
All prices include GST, postage and handling.

CARD NO.

EXPIRY DATE: /   CCV: AMOUNT: $

PURCHASER'S NAME: SIGNATURE:

Subscribe online at **quarterlyessay.com/subscribe** • Freecall: 1800 077 514 • Phone: 03 9486 0288
Email: subscribe@quarterlyessay.com (please do not send electronic scans of this form)